# The Personal Discernment Inventory

## An Instrument for Spiritual Guides

**Brian P. Hall**

**Paulist Press**
**New York, Ramsey, Toronto**

Library of Congress
Catalog Card Number: 80-81325

ISBN: 0-8091-2312-6

Published by Paulist Press
Editorial Office: 1865 Broadway, New York, N.Y. 10023
Business Office: 545 Island Road, Ramsey, N.J. 07446

Printed and bound in the
United States of America

# Contents

# General Introduction

The Personal Discernment Inventory was developed out of ten years of research at the Center for the Exploration of Values and Meaning, in Indianapolis, later to become the Omega Institute. The background to the inventory is a developmental approach to values first described by Hall in a volume published by Paulist Press in 1976: **The Development of Consciousness: A Confluent Theory of Values.** This and an earlier work, **Value Clarification as Learning Process** (Paulist Press, 3 volumes, 1973), stress values as the underpinning of emotional and spiritual growth of each individual.

The most recent works published by Hall with Tonna and Thompson see the individual as person and system. He is always individual, developing in community whatever that community may be. These two volumes are then a background reference to the inventory. They are: **God's Plans for Us: A Practical Strategy for Communal Discernment of**

**Spirits** by Brian Hall and Benjamin Tonna, and **Leadership Through Values: Study of Personal and Organizational Development** by Brian Hall with Helen Thompson, and with William Zierdt as consultant.

The purpose of the inventory is to provide guidelines to individuals and counselors for personal and spiritual growth by enabling a person to see his development through the eyes of the values and priorities that he lives and has lived by. Our values are developmental and as such indicate our present level of growth, where we have come from, and the possibilities for our future.

Our value patterns also point to and clarify the leadership styles we live by. Values and leadership style in turn give even clearer readouts on the skills we have and, more importantly, the skills we need to develop.

Further, the instrument is basically a tool for communal discernment. My level of growth is an indicator, together with my skills, of my stage of ethical and spiritual development. All this information becomes a picture of who I am in value and priority. Consequently, it becomes a measure of how I get along with certain people and identifies persons I am likely to have difficulty with. Put in personal terms it becomes: "Where am I going to be most happy and productive in living out my chosen values?" This is a question of discernment, and it is communal in that what I choose to do is going to affect other people.

Finally the inventory is a tool for spiritual growth. As such the instrument enables a person to get a whole-life perspective on himself; it is not simply for emotional analysis or life career planning. Consequently, many have found the inventory particularly useful when dovetailed with other instruments that have to do with mental health, career and education.

# Whom Is It For?

First it is an adult inventory to aid persons in becoming more conscious of their life-development patterns and to guide them toward decisions that will be value-laden, integrated and creatively growthful for them and those to whom they are related.

More specifically it has been designed to aid persons in executive and management leadership positions. The inventory with its whole-life approach enables the recipient to see in perspective such things as work and home life, play and maintenance, pressure and contemplation. It places success and achievement in relationship to one's own aspired-to values; and, if one wishes, it compares one's value priorities and ethical style with other gospel and creative viewpoints. Finally it flushes out crises and guides one to possible avenues of solution. Professional counselors, personnel guidance counselors and trainers in human-relations work will find this particularly helpful.

Lastly, this is an instrument for spiritual growth. It is an inventory designed for personal and communal discernment of spirits. Professional religious leadership will find this an invaluable aid in spiritual diagnosis and guidance. The instrument has been tested for a number of years in the screening of candidates for the ministry and postulants and novices in religious communities.

Although the inventory can be used for self-analysis, it is much more beneficial when it is used with a trained individual who understands something of the dynamics of human behavior.

# Background Theory

Behind the inventory and its method is the assumption that our lives are guided and motivated by values. Values, by definition, are those major priorities that I choose to act on that creatively enhance my life and the lives of those with whom I am associated. Further, all of life is developmental and, as a result, our priorities change, leading us to live by different value choices as we mature and grow. This assumption led to the development of an eight-stage sequence of life growth—four phases, with two stages (A and B) for each phase. Each stage describes a different level of spiritual maturity and points to different skills necessary for further growth to occur.

Details of the theory are available in the books already mentioned. The following is a brief overview and reminder for those familiar with the material:

The Personal Discernment Inventory first looks at the assumptions that each of us has about his or her life and examines the day-to-day behavior that these assumptions lead to. Values are drawn out from this behavior with the help of a "value list." This should always be done with a partner or guide to increase objectivity. The instrument leads the recipient to a minimum of fifteen values to be examined. In biblical terms these will be seen as signs of charisms that say something about one's life and one's vocation or calling in that life. Fifteen value priorities can be ordered in a thousand different ways, some creative, some possibly destructive. Discernment of spirits is the process of reading these signs in order to discover God's plans for us—not his **plan,** but his possible **plans** for us. In secular humanitarian terms, the outcome is urgent, for the value patterns we choose are our "I Am." In order to be faithful to this sign of "the within" we need to look at what our future demands if we are to maximize our potential.

Before continuing, we need to understand that values are patterns of maturing behavior known as the **phase theory of values:**

**Phase I, stages A and B.** This is the most basic level of development. It is evidenced in the first two or three years of life or a state of being where the individual is totally dependent on others for existence. The world in phase one is a mystery over which the individual has no control. The self is at the center, and moral choice is dictated by what physically satisfies the individual.

At stage A, satisfaction comes through survival in the environment on a day-to-day basis. Naturally, the values the person lives by are limited to self-centeredness, self-preservation, wonder as awe and fate, food/warmth/shelter and safety/survival.

At stage B the person is a little more mature, has acquired a few skills to offset the brutality of day-to-day survival or, in the case of a child, has moved from purely physical needs to emotional needs that are physically related. The values now are such priorities as: self-delight, security rather than preservation, affection/physical, economics as profits.*

**Phase II, stages A and B.** In phase two the world is no longer seen as alien and hostile, but a place in which to belong and succeed. Moral choices as to what is right and what is wrong are now based on social rather than physical needs. Priorities reflect what the phase two person thinks society will approve of. The authority of stage A will be a direct authority, such as parent, teacher or boss. Stage B authority is still external but a little more lofty and distant, such as "the board" or even the Bible.

Stage A values are ones that are marked by the need to belong. Examples are: family/belonging, self/world, being liked, obedience/duty and tradition.

At stage B the more personal values of the A stage become institutionalized, reflecting the need to be competent

---

* A complete list of values at each stage is to be found on page 31 of the inventory.

and successful in the world, as follows: self-competence/confidence, work/labor, competition, achievement/success, play/leisure, education as certification, management and law as rule.

**Phase III, stages A and B.** Rather than a world that is given, phase three persons perceive the world as "creation in process" to which they are invited to make a contribution. Moral choice for the first time is shaped out of conscience, out of personal decision and creative criticism. The self is motivated for the first time from within by a need to express insights, to be his own self, to direct his own life, and to own one's ideas and enterprises.

Stage A is a radical departure from the other-directedness of phase II B with its heavy atmosphere of institutional duty and obligation. Although it is a reaction to the second phase, stage A is highly independent and even self-seeking at times as a new inner world is discovered. The values at this stage are such priorities as: independence, equality/liberation, service/vocation, sharing/listening/trust, law as guide rather than rule, self-directedness and empathy.

In stage B the values become institutionalized and as a consequence more complex. Briefly, the person discovers that true independence is a by-product of cooperation and interdependence. It is a period of exceptional spiritual growth, as the person gets a practical glance at the vision of the world in its wholeness. But to maintain such a vision, values of contemplation and cooperation have to be enacted. A selection of stage B values are: art/beauty as pure value, human dignity, education/knowledge/insight, contemplation, intimacy, justice, accountability/mutual responsibility, and corporation/construction/new order.

**Phase IV, stages A and B.** It is here that the individual's perception of the world changes dramatically. For the first time self is transcended and the person makes all choices and actions based on "we" rather than "I." The consciousness has expanded so that these persons think globally and even cosmically. Individuals are always seen as a part of a greater whole, experienced in such a way as to enhance the beauty of individuals as they act and are acted upon interdependently. The moral imperative here is to reshape the earth and take authority for the created order, to grow in intimacy and union with persons and God at the same time. It is these two dimensions that form stages A and B in this fourth phase. Again A is the personalist dimension, and B its technological outcome.

The value priorities experienced by the few who attain phase four A are: interdependence, truth/wisdom/intuitive insight, personal harmony, intimacy and solitude as unitive, community/personalist, synergy, and word. Since this in fact is a higher level of consciousness and maturity, the value words themselves often seem to be technical. A reference in this regard would be: **The Development of Consciousness: A Confluent Theory of Values** by Brian P. Hall (Paulist Press, New York, 1976).

In stage four B we have: ecority (a combination of ecology, technology, personal authority and harmony)/beauty/aesthetics, harmony/system, transcendence/global confluence, convivial tools, intermediate technology, macro-economics.

**Skills and levels of leadership.** In the stages of value development, patterns emerge that are helpful to us as we seek to understand what is implied by having a certain set of values at a given stage of development. First, as we experience our own value patterns, one finds that they always span three or four stages. This is natural since we are in a stage of growth wherever we are. This span will be an indicator for us of the motion or movement in our lives at this time. But now, as we push this logic a little further, we discover that within this span there is much to be discerned.

We shall use the terms **act, choice** and **vision. Act** is the group of values that appear at the lower end of our developmental schema. If, for example, our values spanned phase II B to III B, a grouping in phase II would arbitrarily be called **act.** These are the bottom-line values that we have had the most experience with. Consequently they would normally describe that place where I have the most skills. Sometimes, however, they describe and point to serious skill deficiencies that I need to take care of if I am to grow. For example, a very mature leader might lack certain but essential management skills that need to be learned if he or she is to be effective.

**Vision** is that value cluster at the highest end of the scale and is consequently a more accurate reading of what I aspire to, rather than what I am actually able to perform. **Choice,** then, is the middle cluster and indicative of the values that I am presently struggling with, and the values that probably need the highest skill application. The purpose of seeing our values this way is to enable us to be realistic about our behavior, and not to confuse vision with where in fact we are now.

**Leading and being.** We all lead in that we all influence the growth and development of others around us, positively or negatively. Leading then is developing. But how we lead, and to what degree we influence others, depends on our level of development. Whether our influence is good or bad depends on our spiritual integration at each level. This spiritual integration is in turn intimately related to skill development because there is a continuing dialectic through life between the internalization of skills and the development of consciousness.

**The four skills.** In order for integrated development to occur in the mature adult, four separate skill areas must be nurtured. This becomes particularly important when we realize that values are in fact also inventories of skills. Therefore certain values would not be developed by an individual unless the right skills were also developed. The four skills are as follows:

**1. Instrumental skills**—ability with intelligence and manual dexterity that enables one to be professional and competent. These are the trained skills of a trade or profession.

**2. Interpersonal skills**—the ability to act with generosity and understanding toward others, that flows from a knowledge of self, and enhances person-to-person communication. It is the ability to communicate with feelings in addition to reason.

**3. Imaginal skills**—ability to initiate new ideas and to take data beyond quantification and logic to the development of new concepts or courses of action. Each of us has an imagination, but imaginal skills provide for the mature use of this faculty to create the new by integrating in fresh ways **instrumental** and **interpersonal** skills.

**4. Systems skills**—the ability to plan and design change in whole systems, such as institutions and bodies of knowledge. It is the ability to act wholistically based on the prior capacity to see how the parts relate to the whole; to see, for example, how one individual's creativity and problems affect the totality of a specific institution. Systems skills arise out of a peculiar blend of imagination, sensitivity to others and professional competence which is in fact the integration of the three other skills.

**Levels of leadership.** The following diagram illustrates the seven levels of leadership development:

| LEADER STAGE | SKILL AND PHASE RANGE LEVEL | WORLD VIEW | LEADER STYLE | FOLLOWER STYLE |
|---|---|---|---|---|
| 1 | I | World as Alien "Alienated Man" | Autocrat Tyrant Dictator | Oppressed Total Dependence |
| 2 | Ib IIa | World as Survival Problem "Preservative Man" | Godfather Benevolent Dictator | Blind Obedient Servant (Means But No End) |
| 3 | II | World as Problem "Organization Man" | Organization Man (Executive) Benevolent Paternalist | Dedicated Servant Organization Loyalist |
| 4 | IIb IIIa | World as Meaning Maker "Communal Man" | Laissez-faire Clarifier Supporter | Leader-Follower Are Confused (Identity Seeker) |
| 5 | III | World as Invention "Independent Man" | Charismatic (Weber) Facilitative Democrat Carpetbagger | Intermediate Peer Participation |
| 6 | IIIb IVa | World as Cooperative Venture "Creator Man" | Leader as Servant Collegial Leadership Interdependent Administration | Collegial Participation |
| 7 | IV | World as Mystery Cared For "Man as Prophet" | Leadership Vision | |

Leadership here is understood to be an expression of the developmental history of the person in relationship to the primary institutions he is related to as a person of influence. Early on in life the institution will be the family, at a later point it will be school, and finally our place of employment and vocation. Our value choices, our present stage of valuing, describe and dictate our leadership style. Our leadership style then becomes a description of how someone working with me or under me is going to feel—the follower style is set by the leadership style. These then in turn describe a world view to which both the follower and the leaders are jointly related.

The leadership diagram relates the phase of development (second column) to the leader level. The particular phase designates all the values that lie behind that leader level. Also, each leader level indicates the way in which the four skills develop and relate to the values. In order to illustrate this further, let us review the seven levels of leadership more closely:

**Level 1: The alienated man.** Phase I values such as self-preservation, security, and safety lie behind this leader's style. The world is alien and people are not to be trusted. Consequently the leader is an autocrat trusting no one, making the follower in extreme cases an oppressed, mistreated individual. This is an appropriate style when the world is in fact alien, as it is at the initiation of a new business or a new mission. Developmentally it is necessary for everyone to experience difficult times and make sense out of them. As such it also reflects that time in life when I must learn the most basic of skills—it is then the initiation of **instrumental skills.** Early on in life learning to read and count were basic survival skills; later on it is the basics of our profession that we need to learn.

**Level 2: The preservative man.** Phase Ib and IIa values such as security and affection are now mixed with items like family/belonging, self-worth, being liked, obedience/duty, competition and tradition. The autocrat is softened with the family orientation, giving us a leader as benevolent dictator. The follower is not oppressed but an obedient believer. The essential skills are still **instrumental** with a stress on rote learning and knowing how to learn— how to ask when you do not know how to do something.

**Level 3: The organization man.** Phase II values are now predominant with the personal needs of self-worth, family/belonging and tradition mixed in with the institutional value priorities of self-competence/confidence, work/labor, achievement/success, management, economics/success,

13

education as certification and administration. The benevolent dictator now becomes the executive as benevolent paternalist. Unlike the previous two styles he listens and takes into account what the follower says, as long as it benefits the organization. He and the follower are dedicated organization people. Management is now the operative word, and therefore the skills are people skills. It is at this stage and the one following that **interpersonal skills** are developed. It is here that minimal skills in administration must be nurtured.

**Level 4: The communal man.** Phase IIb and IIIa values spell crisis. Institutional IIb priorities like management, achievement/success and administration/control are in conflict with the strong self-developmental values of IIIa such as independence, self-actualization, equality/liberation, service/vocation, sharing/listening/trust and self-directedness. Often caught between concern for people and feelings and concern for institutional imperatives, a laissez-faire style emerges which is supportive but indecisive. As one looks at the values it is evident that the primary skill area is **interpersonal.** However, it is precisely at this level that **imaginal skills** begin to develop. This is not simply the ability to see alternatives, to imagine, but it is the ability to take new and disparate data and synergize them into new creative initiatives. It is the active imagination at this level that integrates the other two skills, giving the person for the first time a system perspective. This crisis stage is easily overcome if minimal skill development at all three skill areas occurs, moving the person to the next level.

**Level 5: Independent man.** This is a full phase III with values such as independence, self-actualization, empathy and service/vocation at the early part of the phase, and priorities such as human dignity, contemplation/asceticism, accountability/mutual responsibility, intimacy, justice, and corporation/construction/new order at the end of the phase. At the skill level, what has occurred is the full development of the **imaginal skill** which in turn has integrated **instrumental** and **interpersonal** skills, causing a shift in consciousness to a system perspective. This level then marks the initiation of **system skills.** This is a period of reorientation, as new powers and a new sense of leadership ability are tested out. "Democratic" and "charismatic" describe the leader at this level.

**Level 6: The creator man.** Phase IVa vision is now mixed with a IIIb set of priorities. Values of human dignity, education as insight, contemplation, and accountability/mutual responsibility are developed by phase IV values such as interdependence, truth/wisdom/intuitive insight, intimacy and solitude as unitive, and a personal sense of harmony with a world that is now perceived as international. This leader, seeing the wider vision, and having maximum skills at the corporate and the interpersonal level, becomes leader as servant when the skills are integrated.

**Level 7: Man as prophet.** The values here are phase IV priorities as follows: interdependence, truth and harmony (personal) in IVa and macro-economics, convivial tools/intermediate technology, transcendence and ecority/beauty/aesthetic in IVb. The leader here is not so much an executive leader as a spokesman for global harmony and wider moral perspective. He or she is leader as prophet.

**Patterns and spiritual development.** The purpose of the Personal Discernment Inventory is to allow you to raise questions, make choices and act with some confidence in ways that will creatively affect your wholistic development. Wholistic growth is what Thomas Merton and a host of others down through the ages have termed spiritual development. Once you are clear on what your values are, and what you mean by them (Part I of the inventory) you will be able to see patterns of growth for yourself.

We have already seen that our values are a developmental pattern, pointing to past experience (act), future possibility (vision), and what I am working on now (choice). The instrument will help you see yourself historically and enable you to raise questions so as to discern the meaning. It will point to your present skills and how they relate to your values. From this you will be able to discern specific directions and work out the details of what it is you need to learn in the near future in order to develop the values you have identified. Additionally we have looked briefly at how value priorities say something directly about our leadership style and ability. Part IV of the instrument will help us see our own unique set of leadership patterns.

Apart from what has already been mentioned there are two other significant patterns that will be dealt with in the inventory. First is the dimension of time. Values are chosen in the context of how much time we have to spend on them. For example, if I work sixteen hours a day I will have little time for play or play values such as contemplation or intimacy. I will not have time for family. My time will relate only to work values such as management or administration. This set of patterning is called **quality perspective** and appears in Part II.

Finally, but by no means least, is the **ethical dimension.** For some, especially those who work in spiritual direction or those who are concerned with hiring for high-level executive positions, this will be a most essential piece of information. How I choose my values and how they cluster will point to the ethical style that I am most comfortable with as an overall life pattern. My present stage of development is a clear indication of how I make ethical choices, how my conscience works. But additionally the overall values I choose point to a style that is uniquely mine, and one to which the natural order of things calls me. To operate another way would be out of character and probably cause me some unhappiness. It is therefore critical to my growth to know what my ethical style is.

Basically there are four ethical ways which the inventory points out: 1. Institutional/communal; 2. Ideological or eschatological; 3. Service or agapitical; and 4. Dialogical or legal approach. They are in a sense indicators of my vocational inclination, but they are also clear orientations toward living that lead us in different directions, with different interests, and consequently different ethical styles.

## What Lies Behind the Inventory

The inventory has some of its own methods of education, along with a few presuppositions that would be helpful to review at this time. The inventory is not a test or even a way of simply collecting data. It is much more; it is a **process** of learning and growing in consciousness about one's life in relationship to the lives around us. It is the study of one's "self system" in relationship to all the other systems with which one interacts. The process is deliberate and has four parts to it that continually cycle and repeat themselves throughout the inventory. The four processes that make up the experience as a whole are: contemplation, generation, reflection and construction.

**Contemplation,** as the initiation of the process, is the sitting with oneself or another and seeing beyond externals and even specific behavior to the values and priorities that lie beyond. It implies being with another in silence, actively listening without judgment, and seeking to see the wonder and beauty of being itself—whether it be mine or some other person's. For the person of faith it becomes ultimately encounter with the Other, the ground of all being.

**Generation** is the active consequence of the contemplative act. Concretely, when I observe your behavior, listen to your assumptions, I suddenly see all the value

16

priorities that lie behind them. Both priorities can be ordered in a hundred, even a thousand different ways! This is in fact the generation of possibility—an imaginal gift for me to explore.

**Reflection** is the beginning of choice; it is the process of sifting through the possibilities that have been generated through contemplation. Reflection then is actively discerning what possibilities are the most creative, most life-giving for me and those around me at this time.

**Construction** is the choosing and acting on a specific possibility. In this inventory it is the process of contracting for specific skill development or changes in one's life-style.

The four processes are contained in each part of the inventory, and reflect a general process of valuing. Behind the instrument, or rather the theory that supports it, are a number of presuppositions that it would be well to clarify. It is presupposed that:

1. Life is developmental in all its aspects and that the attainment of a more full and conscious life, a more spiritually whole life, demands a hierarchy of development in some areas of that life. More specifically, certain values require the prior development of other values in order for them to be actualized in our behavior. For example, the value of empathy requires the prior development of self-worth not to be subverted into sympathy. Skills are also developed hierarchically. Management requires prior skills in mathematics and administration. High levels of contemplation require skills in imagination and play. Even in the scale of leadership, skills in survival are necessary before one delegates one's authority to others with trust.

2. Life is struggle. In each stage of our life we are pulled simultaneously to both ends of the value scale. Phase one has its biological drives and necessities, the need to survive, the need to control and the need to be secure and comfortable (narcissism). The pull at the other end is to self-actualization with the will to create, to find intimacy and union, to take authority for the created order (ecority). To be conscious and aware of the higher values and yet to submit to the behavioral necessities of the earlier phases is to choose death rather than life. It is the classical battle between good and evil, especially when choosing the higher good puts us in opposition to those who normally support and sustain us.

3. Life is a developing consciousness which contains within itself a moral imperative to create rather than destroy, to seek meaning and knowledge rather than security, to strive after intimacy and union with man and God rather than personal power and self-love.

4. The seven levels of leadership reflect these first three suppositions. Leadership is simply the ability to influence others. But a person with phase four consciousness can still decide to be a tyrant, a false prophet, using all his skills of enlightenment to control, protect what he has and use others to support his need for power. History is filled with such persons. So it is that development, although a fact, is not a guarantee against the necessity of struggle to develop in an integrated and whole way. (For a fuller discussion of this, see the works referred to on page 5.) This struggle to be whole is precisely the moral imperative reflected in the leader style as servant (level 6) and prophet (level 7). The concept of servant is the antithesis of control and self-service. A prophet in the Judeo-Christian tradition at least implies one who is fully conscious and aware of God's presence and so in Tillich's terms becomes the medium for God's Word. But whether one is a person of faith or not, the prophet still becomes the medium of revelation exposing the purpose of history and man's place within it. In the faith context, this is salvation history and what is revealed is God's plans for us.

# Using the Inventory*

The inventory can be used for personal discernment and spiritual growth, by counselors in giving guidance, in seminars and retreats, and as an instrument for hiring and selection purposes.

**1. Personal use of the inventory for spiritual review and growth.** Personal growth and development are always a question of discernment. It is always a question of being able to discern and act on the "right" course of action. For the counselor this is always directed toward the happy and creative life; for the spiritual guide it is seeking that direction on our pilgrimage that is in accordance with God's plans for us. This is difficult if not impossible to do without objective help. Therefore if you are using this instrument personally, do it with someone else that you trust. If you have a family, have the whole family (over seven or eight years of age) do it, and discern together as a community. But always be open to bringing in someone to help you who has a professional background—a priest, minister, sister or counselor. When you need assistance, the most important thing is to get someone you trust and who is competent in guidance.

---

* A fuller explanation of the use of the inventory is available on cassette tapes from Paulist Press.

**2. Use of the inventory by counselors and spiritual guides.** The instrument is a process, and as such goes beyond usefulness as a tool for quality diagnosis. It has in my own experience provided the framework for up to fifteen interviews, with the clients using the instrument at home between sessions. It is important to understand the value theory that lies behind the instrument's design before using it with clients. Please see page 00 for suggested readings.

Training and consultation is available in regard to the inventory and value-based discernment processes. For information please write the author at:

Graduate Humanities Department
University of Santa Clara
Santa Clara, California 95053

For inquiries in Europe or the Middle East please contact:
The Reverend Benjamin Tonna
Omega Institute
45 Buskett Road
Rabat, Malta (Europe)

For inquiries in Asia and Africa please contact:
The Reverend Anthony D'Souza
St. Xavier College,
Bombay 400 001, India

**3. As a tool for teaching and retreats.** Maximal use of the inventory is in these settings a framework for growth. The minimal time the instrument can be completed in is about twenty-four hours. Parts I and II can be completed in twelve hours or a weekend retreat. Let us consider three settings: the classroom or adult-education experience, the weekend retreat, the five-day retreat.

**Use of the inventory in a teaching setting.** In this setting the inventory is not sufficient on its own, and must be supplemented by content or a theoretical base. The readings suggested on page 5 will begin this process for you. If the setting is religious, **God's Plans for Us** should be used as well as the other texts.

It is my experience that the inventory does not lend itself well to a teaching structure that is limited to one-hour blocks of time. The setting should be seminar type, of about three hours in duration for eight to ten sessions. The students or adult participants need to work for the most part in dyads or in threes. This way a certain objectivity is preserved and participants acquire practice in helping others.

Suggested use of the inventory in this format is as follows:

**Session 1.** Content: Discussion of what is understood by anassumption and what is understood by value.*
Practice: Writing, sharing and prioritizing of assumptions with a partner. Beginning to share behaviors related to the assumptions. (See Inventory, Part I.)

**Session 2.** Content: The value theory and the development of consciousness as the phases of value development.
Practice: Sharing of behaviors from the original assumptions. Converting the behavior into values. Choosing and prioritizing the values.

Session 3. Content: Review of the theory and its relationship to other writings on development.
Practice: Defining the values and sharing experiences with your partner (Inventory, Part I).

**Session 4.** Content: Discussion of priorities as act, choice and vision. Discussion of the four skills and their relationship to different values.
Practice: Constructing and sharing of one's consciousness track. Discussion of the questions of discernment (Inventory, Part II).

**Session 5.** Content: Discussion of the relationship between the values and quality time and one's ethical stance.
Practice: Prioritizing one's goals and objectives. Relating one's values to skills, quality time and ethical stance. Discerning through sharing with one's partner.

**Session 6.** Content: Detailed discussion of the process of skill development.
Practice: Development of skill inventories (Inventory, Part II).

**Session 7.** Content: Discussion of the seven levels of leadership development.
Practice: Continuation of the development of a program in skill development. Initial discussion of leadership questions (Inventory, Part III and IV).

**Session 8.** Content: Discussion of what is meant by contract and its implication for the spiritual life. Discussion of the concept of ongoing development and evaluation.
Practice: Completion and sharing of the contracts.

**Use of the inventory for a weekend retreat.** Since the retreat concept includes a time of quiet reflection and prayer, only a part of the inventory should be used. If the retreat were to last from 5 P.M. on Friday through 4 P.M. on Sunday, there would be sufficient time for the first four sessions illustrated above (that is to say, to the completion of

---

* See suggested references on page 5.

the questions on discernment). A suitable conclusion would be to use the last hour on a partial completion of the contract (Inventory, Part IV).

**Use of the inventory in a five-day retreat.** I have included this option because it is the optimal condition for completion of the total instrument in a relaxed manner. Using the format described above, sessions 1 to 4 would be completed in days one and two. Sessions 5 and 6 would be completed on day three and until noon of day four. Sessions 7 and 8 are then given plenty of reflection time until noon of the fifth day. A normal format for me has been to begin at nine on Monday, finishing after lunch on Friday.

An interesting approach and one that is productive is to have the first session each day at nine finishing before noon. The Eucharist would be at four o'clock followed by an agape supper. The afternoon would be in silence or counseling. The evening session would begin at six. On the last day the Eucharist would be at noon followed by lunch to complete the retreat. Often we will use the offering at the final Eucharist to share our contracts and to say a few words of thanks and good-bye.

**4. Use of the inventory in selection and hiring procedures.** In this section we shall consider the use of the inventory in the selection of candidates for the ministry and priesthood; its parallel use in the novitiate in religious communities; its use in industry and churches as a tool for personnel selection and promotion and as a tool for management supervision.

**The use of the inventory in selection of candidates for the ministry and the priesthood.** A great deal of my experience in this regard, and it was experience that had a direct influence on the development of the Personal Discernment Inventory, was with the Episcopal Church. The committee that deals with candidates who wish to become priests or enter a seminary to test their vocation is BACAM—the Bishop's Advisory Commission on Applicants for the Ministry. However, the problems encountered in selection were no different than I encountered in my consultations with numerous other churches. The churches consulted ranged from a number of Roman Catholic dioceses and religious communities right across the board to a number of our evangelical brethren such as the Church of the Nazarene and the Church of God.

In my own denomination, selection has often been a problem, especially in the last decade when there have been far more candidates than positions available. Quite apart from basic questions as to exactly what ministry is, the selection process tended to utilize testing which stressed that the candidate was not emotionally or physically sick. It came out of a medical model, not a spiritual one. Typically the candidate would have a psychiatric interview, a medical examination, a series of psychological tests (stressing mental health, intelligence and vocational inclination) and then a series of interviews with the bishop and his selection committee. He or she would additionally have to have had a sound record of performance in the local congregation.

For the most part such a process worked well when there was a shortage of candidates and when the level of sophistication of the laity was not what it is now. Now we are in a situation where the minister is not guaranteed a full-time job and where strong imaginative leadership is called for. This means the churches need persons with the kind of spiritual qualities that psychological testing and interviews do not help with. Hence the development of the Personal Discernment Inventory—not as an answer to all these problems, God forbid, but as a way of making fewer mistakes. The inventory aids selection committees in asking the right questions and seeking helpful information, and at the same time it gives helpful guidance to the candidate.

The inventory is not a substitute for the other interviews, data-collecting and testing; it is a supplement to them. It is also often a corrective to the other data. Since the inventory takes a long time to administer and process, we suggest the candidates meet as a group for one full day, completing sessions 1, 2 and 4 (see page 20). They then go away for a week and complete the rest of the inventory as best they can. On the return, they enter a second overnight retreat interview conference, spending the first day in groups finishing, discussing and reflecting on the instrument. The candidate then reflects on and suggests questions about his own life that would be helpful to the committee. Finally, in the interview he shares his contract and anything else of the inventory he or she wishes. It is at this point only that the committee then poses its questions.

Two suggestions in regard to the process: One—never have an interviewing board or committee follow this procedure unless the majority of the board has itself undergone the process (the inventory). Minimally they must all be open to such a process, nonjudgmental, with at least one person who has had thorough exposure to the instrument. Two—when you are dealing with married rather than celibate clergy, try to involve the husband or wife in the process. If they are single then the issue of the sacrament of marriage or the reality of celibacy must be equally dealt with.

The inventory raises a number of questions automatically about ministry that other testing procedures do not. First of all the selection committee must be clear about its own view of ministry. For example, is ministry primarily priesthood? Is it primarily sacramental, of the word, institutional, or congregational? My point is the committee must be clear about its own stance and make this clear to the candidate. The value clusters that the candidate has will illustrate levels of maturity, styles of ministry, needed skills, ethical style and leadership capacity. These will appear as manifestations rather than matters of theological discussion—and as such the candidate is exposing him or herself at a deep level. Care therefore must be taken to use this inventory not simply as a tool for screening and judgment, but also as a tool for guidance and spiritual advice. Once the candidate's pastoral style is clear the committee can give guidance and advice on how it may be best actualized; secondarily then comes the question whether such a style is appropriate for this diocese or congregation at this time.

**The use of the inventory in religious life.** It is probably clear from the last section that the inventory has direct applicability in the election of novices to the professed life in religious communities. It might also be used for pre-novitiate training and selection as a way to introduce people to the style of a particular community.

We have suggested to most communities that they use the instrument as a tool for training and education. In this way the novice master or mistress can also share his or her values. By the time the course is over both the novice and the director will know if the person is going to be happy in community—or at least they will be realistic about the problems this person might encounter.

**The use of the inventory as a tool for personnel selection, promotion and supervision, both in industry and the churches.**

**1. As a tool for personnel selection and promotion.** This is just as applicable to industry as it is to the churches. First of all I have placed selection and promotion together because the inventory is a process instrument—an instrument of evaluation. By going through the process each year, one updates the inventory. It would take no more than a day to review, since our values do not change a great deal from year to year, although their quality will. Again such a process is as helpful to the person doing the instrument as to the bishop or, in the case of industry, the personnel officer.

The inventory gives quality information and is therefore invaluable in the hiring of top executive personnel where ethics and leadership ability become of high concern. The instrument is of particular usefulness in the calling of a new minister to a congregation. Lay people are often intimidated by religious persons in authority and do not like to ask gritty questions about spiritual matters. In the secular world, if you have value data on all personnel, you can now see an individual in relationship to the whole system, and hopefully make fewer mistakes in hiring and placement. As an example, Part II of the inventory points out that a person who has value clusters that are more than one stage apart from another person's value clusters will probably not get along very well in a peer team relationship. These kinds of problems and analyses will often require technical consultation, in which case it would be wise to get outside help when necessary.*

**2. The use of the inventory in supervisory guidance.** This use of the instrument in supervision is the same as any guidance process, except that the purpose and goals are limited by the institution. A bishop talking to a clergyman, no matter how good a pastor he is, is limited by the fact that he is the employer of that priest to some degree at least. However, the instrument is still very valuable in that it is a great aid in troubleshooting and the guidance and the decision-making that comes out of that.

Another way in which the inventory is an aid in supervision is when the supervisor has a large number of supervisees. It is then an aid to the recall of quality and often complex information. Finally, the instrument is helpful in team-casing. When the supervisor or pastor is working on a team that has a common personnel problem, then the discussion is enhanced by quality information. In brief, we are less likely to make serious mistakes with this kind of added data.

# Conclusion

The Personal Discernment Inventory is a way of exploring one's value priorities as a means and an aid to discernment. It is ultimately a spiritual quest in that you seek to look for a

---

* See page 19 for addresses of persons who can give consultation or inform you of the closest person in your area.

moment at least at whole persons on their individual journeys. I did not pretend to make a perfect instrument for this end, but only a process that would aid the would-be counselor in making fewer silly mistakes. We will always continue to make mistakes, but what we aim to do here is make fewer, especially when we are making them for someone else!

On the darker side, we know that we have many false prophets to contend with in this world. How do we know people will not use this instrument and the information they get to their own ends? How do we know that industry, even the churches, won't computerize the information and use it without any regard for privacy and respect of persons?

The fact is that there are no safeguards that are foolproof. When the theory of values is rightly understood, and not used with blatant disregard for its structure, it moves persons toward wholeness and health and not the other way around. This of course refers to the individual use of the instrument.

The danger is that persons will misinterpret its use for others, or even make decisions about them, for what the data say. The first point to remember is that the instrument as it is presently structured gives only a limited amount of information to the untrained eye. Therefore extensive use of the instrument requires training and supervision. In our training and consultation we make a point to deal extensively with the ethics of the use of this kind of instrument.

Throughout the introduction we have stressed that this is a process instrument. IT WOULD BE INAPPROPRIATE AND WRONG TO USE THE INVENTORY AS A WAY OF GAINING INFORMATION ON A PERSON WITHOUT FULL CONSULTATION AND OPEN DISCUSSION WITH THAT PERSON.

In this regard we urge persons who want to use the instrument for personnel selection and data collection to acquire the appropriate training and consultation. For assistance please write the author.*

Finally the inventory is an aid to discernment, much in the same way that the exercises of Ignatius of Loyola are an aid. They are an aid to persons seeking growth for themselves and others, in order to attempt to construct a world that we will all be proud to live in. It is then a very small piece of a larger spiritual heritage—one to which we are all called.

At this point, then, I invite you to use the inventory, to explore the inner world of value, priorities and ultimate potential for you and those whom you care about.

---

* The address is to be found on page 19.

# Introduction

The Personal Discernment Inventory (PDI) is an instrument designed to help the pastor or executive become more conscious of his assumptions about his and others' leader-management styles. It assumes an awareness of stages of value development and leadership stages (see background theory in the General Introduction).

Following an analysis of leadership assumptions, the PDI will examine behavior and the values that lie behind them. Here you will accept or challenge your own priorities in terms of what your leadership style ought to be within the limited framework of your present situation.

Next your values and priorities will be examined developmentally for the purpose of review and reflection. You will then be able to say "This is where I am now; this is good." With this knowledge, you will be free to ask, "Where do I want to go from here?"

Finally the PDI will begin to look at the use of the **skills,** the **time** and the **ethic** that lie behind your values.

The usual way of using this instrument is to be paired with one other person to insure more objectivity and to become familiar with the methodology. In a framework of confidence, PDI introduces you to yourself in a new way and will enable you to:

1. Plan better for your future.
2. Set measured goals and objectives for yourself more clearly.
3. Relate your goals and objectives to your institution's goals and objectives.
4. Diagnose more clearly skills needed in yourself and others.
5. See the relationship between quality-time and management pressure.
6. Look at the ethics of the leadership style you exhibit.

Additionally this instrument was designed to train the leader:

1. To recognize more readily communication problems among personnel who work closely with him.
2. To diagnose more clearly skills needed on his staff.
3. To state clearly value-based goals and objectives of the Church or organization and its leadership.
4. To practice contract accountability.

This instrument is not designed to solve all leadership problems: it will make you more aware of the various components of leadership and give you significant skills that will enable you to make decisions with fewer mistakes.

## General Instructions
### —What to Expect—

**A. Behavior.** Expect to look at your past behavior. You will do this several times and you will be asked to be specific. What did you do? Whom did you do it with? What time and what day was it? In other words, when you mention behavior, be sure to be quite specific.

**B. Detail.** Expect to be careful and detailed and accurate as you fill out the instrument. Don't let anyone hurry you. Use a pencil—you might want to erase occasionally.

**C. Assumption.** Expect to look at the basic assumptions by which you live and act out your life. Don't be surprised if you change them or add new ones after a while—this is an experience that is designed to expand your awareness. Most of us never think about what our assumptions are.

**D. Process.** This is a process instrument and may not make sense to you until it is almost completed. Some steps in the process may seem unnecessary. You may as a result be tempted to short-cut some steps—please don't! Our experience is that all the steps are necessary and will in the long run be helpful.

**E. Learning.** Expect to learn some important things about yourself but be patient in the early stages.

**Part I**

# The Personal Assumption Analysis

## Instructions

An assumption is something taken for granted. It is a basic belief you have about your work, your family, your religion or your life. It contains your most important values and it affects all your decisions.

### Instruction 1

Consider these example assumptions and how they would affect your day-to-day existence:

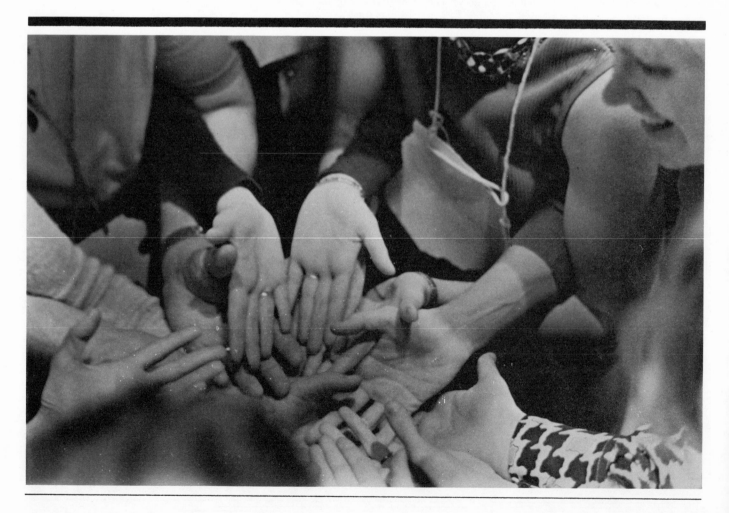

28

1. Work is something I dislike and have to do.
2. My work is the most important thing in my life.
3. People are not to be trusted.
4. Men should work and women should look after the home.
5. My education is the most important thing right now.
6. Living in a nice house and being home on the weekends is important to me.
7. I need basic security.

Consider for a moment what the consequences of some of these might be. What behavior would you expect some of these to lead to?

## Instruction 2

What are the most **important** assumptions you hold about work and your life? Think of six (A, B, C, D, E, and F) and write them down in the first column below.

| Assumption | Priority Listing |
|---|---|
| A. | |
| B. | |
| C. | |
| D. | |
| E. | |
| F. | |

30 min. max.

## Instruction 3

Discuss your assumptions with a partner. Rewrite them if necessary. When you are satisfied with what is written, prioritize them in terms of what is most important, based on your present behavior. Put your priority listing in the last column by indicating its number: 1, 2, 3, 4, 5, or 6. For example, if B is your first priority, put a "1" in the last column.

## Testing Your Assumptions
## Instruction 4 (2.5 hrs. max.)

Having prioritized your assumptions, you will now take the **first four** and examine them through your behavior. **For example,** if an assumption was, "The education of my children is more important than my work," an example behavior might be: "I changed a 5 o'clock appointment with a client last Wednesday to listen to my son Martin's homework problem."

A specific behavior, then, is one that is observable recently in time and place, with nameable persons. The behavior was a specific moment, not a period of time.

For each assumption, starting with your first priority, think of **five** specific and recent (during the last six months) behaviors. Do this with your partner, sharing one of his behaviors at a time; this will enable you to remember behaviors more easily.

Using the forms provided below, write your priority assumption over each box and then list the five behaviors. Order of importance is not required at this stage. Start with your first priority.

**First Assumption**

| |
|---|
| Behavior 1. |
| 2. |
| 3. |
| 4. |
| 5. |

**Second Assumption**

| |
|---|
| Behavior 1. |
| 2. |
| 3. |
| 4. |
| 5. |

**Third Assumption**

| |
|---|
| Behavior 1. |
| 2. |
| 3. |
| 4. |
| 5. |

**Fourth Assumption**

| |
|---|
| Behavior 1. |
| 2. |
| 3. |
| 4. |
| 5. |

## Looking at the Values
## Behind Your Assumptions—Instruction 5
## (20 min. max.)

Your assumptions are described in day-to-day life by the way you live them out—by the way you behave. These specific behaviors you have just listed point in turn to underlying values and priorities, as follows:

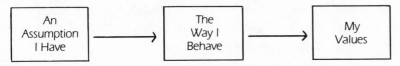

But in my daily living the reverse is true.

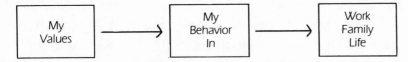

Therefore to be conscious of your values is important, for they then become guides in your behavior toward others at work and at home. They are what motivate you.

A value, then, is a priority I choose and act on that allows me to live productively and happily with myself and others.

Look over carefully the list of values that follow. Which ones do you think are operating in your behavior?

| | | | | |
|---|---|---|---|---|
| 1 Accountability/Mutual Responsibility | 25 Courtesy/Respect | 51 Fantasy/Play | 77 Membership/Institution | 102 Security |
| 2 Achievement/Success | 26 Creativity/Ideation | 52 Food/Warmth/Shelter | 78 Mission/Goals | 103 Sensory Pleasure/Sex |
| 3 Adaptability/Flexibility | 27 Criteria/Rationality | 52 Friendship/Belonging | 79 Obedience/Duty | 104 Service/Vocation |
| 4 Administration/Control | 28 (Self) Delight | 54 Function | 80 Obedience/Mutual Accountability | 105 Sharing/Listening/Trust |
| 5 Affection/Physical | 29 Detachment/Solitude | 55 Generosity/Service | 81 Objectivity | 106 Simplicity/Play |
| 6 Art/Beauty/As pure value | 30 Decision/Initiation | 56 Growth/Expansion | 82 Ownership | 107 Social Affirmation |
| 7 (Self) Assertion | 31 Design/Pattern/Order | 57 Harmony/System | 83 Patriotism/Esteem | 108 Support Peer |
| 8 Being Liked | 32 (Self) Directedness | 58 Health/Personal | 84 Pioneerism/Innovation/Progress | 109 Synergy |
| 9 Being Self | 33 Discovery/Delight | 59 Hierarchy/Propriety/Order | 85 Play/Leisure | 110 Tradition |
| 10 Care/Nurture | 34 Discernment/Communal | 60 Honor | 86 Poverty/Simplicity | 111 Transcendence/Global Conference |
| 11 (Self) Centeredness | 35 Duty/Obligation | 61 Human Dignity | 87 Pluriformity | 112 Truth/Wisdom/Intuitive Insight |
| 12 Communications | 36 Economics/Profit | 62 Independence | 88 Power Authority/Honesty | 113 Unity/Solidarity |
| 13 Community/Personalist | 37 Economics/Success | 63 Instrumentality | 89 Presence/Dwelling | 114 Wonder/Awe/Fate |
| 14 Community/Supportive | 38 Ecority/Beauty/Aesthetics | 64 Integration/Wholeness | 90 (Self) Preservation | 115 Wonder/Curiosity |
| 15 Competition | 39 Education/Certification | 65 Independence | 91 Prestige/Image | 116 Word |
| 16 (Self) Competence/Confidence | 40 Education/Knowledge/Insight | 66 Intimacy | 92 Productivity | 117 Work/Labor |
| 17 Congruence | 41 Efficiency/Planning | 67 Intimacy and Solitude as unitive | 93 Property/Control | 118 Workmanship/Craft |
| 18 Construction/New Order | 42 Empathy | 68 Justice | 94 Recreation/Freesence | 119 Worship/Duty/Creed |
| 19 Contemplation/Asceticism | 43 Equilibrium | 69 Knowledge/Discovery/Insight | 95 Relaxation | 120 (Self) Worth |
| 20 (Self) Control | 44 Equality/Liberation | 70 Law/Guide | 96 Research/Originality/Knowledge | |
| 21 Control/Order/Discipline | 45 Equity/Rights | 71 Law/Rule | 97 Responsibility | |
| 22 Convivial Tool/Intermediate Technology | 46 Ethics/Accountability/Values | 72 Live/Self Actualization | 98 Ritual/Weaning | |
| 23 Cooperation | 47 Evaluation/Self System | 73 Limitation/Celebration | 99 Rule/Accountability | |
| 24 Corporation/Construction/New Order | 48 Expressiveness/Freedom | 74 Loyalty/Respect | 100 Safety/Survival | |
| | 49 Faith/Risk | 75 Macro Economics | 101 Search/Meaning | |
| | 50 Family/Belonging | 76 Management | | |

# Brainstorming Values—
## Instruction 6 (2 hrs. max.)

This exercise is to be done with your partner, not alone. Starting with the first assumption, review your five behaviors and discuss them sufficiently so that the underlying values become obvious.

1. Using the values list, in the first box below write down as many values as you can that could be major values underlying these five behaviors. You should list at least twelve values in less than five minutes.

Brainstorming means you do not discuss or define the values; both you and your partner simply call out the values and write them down.

2. Once you have your values, take pencil and choose the four you feel were **priorities** in the behavior you are examining. Your partner may argue with you—an objective outsider often sees things a little more clearly. The object, however, is for you to come to consensus with your partner on the four most important values reflected in that behavior.

3. Once you have arrived at consensus on four values, prioritize them **based on your behavior** in the side column marked **value priorities.**

4. Now proceed to the other assumptions. When you are finished you will have sixteen values—or less, if there is repetition.

**Assumption One**

| Brainstormed Values | Value Priorities |
|---|---|
| | 1. |
| | 2. |
| | 3. |
| | 4. |

**Assumption Two**

| Brainstormed Values | Value Priorities |
|---|---|
| | 1. |
| | 2. |
| | 3. |
| | 4. |

**Assumption Three**

| Brainstormed Values | Value Priorities |
|---|---|
| | 1. |
| | 2. |
| | 3. |
| | 4. |

**Assumption Four**

| Brainstormed Values | Value Priorities |
|---|---|
| | 1. |
| | 2. |
| | 3. |
| | 4. |

## Defining Your Values—
## Instruction 7 (2.5 hrs. max.)

Value words are symbols of constellations of meaningful experiences that lie behind them. We have dictionaries to limit the meaning an individual might put on a word so as to increase common interpersonal communication. However, a dictionary does not plumb the depth a significant symbol like a value might have for a person; therefore, it is necessary for **you and your partner** to define all the values. If you have values in common **only one definition** is necessary.

In order to define the value, a return to experience of that value is necessary:

1. Discuss the value to be defined for a minute or so.

2. Brainstorm, rapidly writing down specific (moment, time, place and person) experiences you each have had of that value. Example: Human dignity. Brainstorm specific moments when you felt dignified as a person or moments that enabled dignity to occur.

3. After you have a list of eight to ten experiences, group them into common experiences, prioritize them, and write a definition of the value using qualities inherent in the experiences.

Example: Human dignity.

Experiences: (1) My wife greeted me with a kiss last night when I came home from work. Qualities: felt special, belonging.

(2) Daughter made a special meal for me on my birthday. Qualities: forethought, effort, affirmation.

(3) Congratulated George yesterday for successfully completing a job two hours earlier than expected. Qualities: Affirmation of this value to me, appreciation, physical touch.

(4) Gave medical benefits to part-time staff as of the fifteenth of last month. Qualities: Physical security, service for partly employed, justice for less fortunate.

(5) Took an employee personally to the doctor when he broke his finger last week. Qualities: Care, put myself out, put my priorities aside.

**Example definition** going from priority one first: **Human dignity** is that sense of being made to feel you are special and belong by other persons who make a special effort to care for you. It is something that moves beyond home and feelings to the affirmation of persons at work and home, with a concern for physical and emotional well-being, and a sense of justice to all mankind.

This is but one **example.** Once you have defined a value, check the value list to make sure the title of the value is appropriate to the definition. For example, if only the first sentence of the above definition were used, **self-worth** rather than **human dignity** might have been a more accurate title.

This is a skill-building exercise so that ten minutes is the absolute maximum time you need to spend on any definition. Define your ten most important values only at this time. (These are the values which underpin your personal assumptions.)

Write your values definitions down on the list given here.

## Final Value List

**Top ten defined values:**

1. _____
2. _____
3. _____
4. _____
5. _____
6. _____
7. _____
8. _____
9. _____
10. _____

**Remaining values:**

11. _____
12. _____
13. _____
14. _____
15. _____
16. _____

**Spend** fifteen minutes discussing your priorities with your partner.

## Part II

# Personal Value Analysis: The Consciousness Track

## Introduction

**I. Value priorities are developmental.** Some of your values will be more indicative of where you would like to be than where you actually are. These are your aspirations or visions. Other priorities are ones that perhaps you are aware of but for the most part they are taking care of themselves. For example: Family/belonging might be important to you but for the most part you feel this is taken care of. This is what we call act—it is being done already. Finally, there is a large grey area in the middle called **choice** values. These are the value priorities that occupy our minds most of the time but could

use improvement. Empathy, for example, is a value we may try to implement, but perhaps feel we could use more skills in this area. The accompanying diagram will illustrate this further:

# Values As Choice—Act—Vision

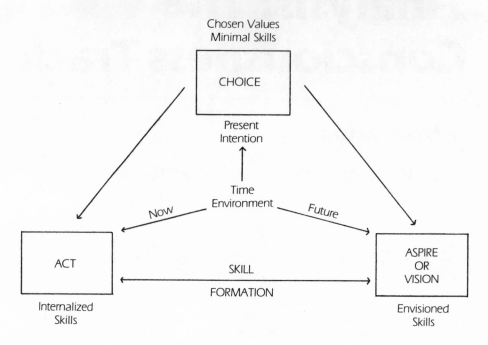

Choice values are the ones I can do when I am not under pressure. But when I am in a new situation or under pressure, I find the values are not internalized sufficiently for me to **act** them out unconsciously. **Act values** are those that are a part of my behavior no matter what the pressure. As we develop the skills of our **choice values** and these priorities become internalized as **act values,** so I grow toward my **vision** or **aspired values.**

**II. Value priorities underlie our goals and objectives.** There are two types of value priorities: long-term priorities or "primary values" and short-term priorities or "means values." For example, **family** is a long-term priority. It is the kind of value that always remains important to us in a conscious way. **Sharing** is a short-term priority because it is skill orientated and once we learn to do it we forget it. It becomes habitual.

The long-term priorities are our **goals.** The short-term priorities are our **objectives**. You will be able to identify which is which by the use of the instrument below.

The purpose of this exercise is to:

1. Help you discover your goals.
2. Help you discover your objectives for the coming year.

3. Enable you to see which are your **vision** or aspired to values, and which are your present **choices.**

4. Enable you to reflect more clearly on your present stage of spiritual development.

## Construction of Your Consciousness Track. Instruction 1 (1 hr. max.)

1. The accompanying (page 38) instrument called a "Consciousness Track" places the original list of 120 values into their 4 phases, or 8 developmental stages. Briefly review this chart.

2. Please note that there are four phases with an "A" stage (white column) and a "B" stage (grey column)—two stages for each phase. Note also there are values at the top of each column—the primary values—and values at the bottom—the means values.

Turn now to your **value list** on page 34 and begin to identify: (1) Which phase and stage each value is in. For example: Empathy IIIa. (2) Which type of value it is: Primary— top column—or Means—bottom of column.

3. Now place all your values on their own consciousness track on page 37, each in its right place—that is, phase stage and at the top or bottom.

**Personal Consciousness Track**

| | I | | | II | | | III | | | IV | |
|---|---|---|---|---|---|---|---|---|---|---|---|
| | A | B | A | | B | A | | B | A | | B |
| **Primary Values — Goals** | | | | | | | | | | | |
| **Means Values — Objectives** | | | | | | | | | | | |

# Consciousness Track

| PHASE I | | PHASE II | | PHASE III | | PHASE IV | |
|---|---|---|---|---|---|---|---|
| **A [Primary]**<br>(Self) Centeredness<br>*(Self) Preservation<br>Wonder/Awe/Fate | **B [Primary]**<br>(Self) Delight<br>*Security | **A [Primary]**<br>(Self) Control<br>**Family/Belonging<br>Fantasy/Play<br>*(Self) Worth | **B [Primary]**<br>Play/Leisure<br>*Self Competence/ Confidence<br>Work/Labor<br>Worship/Duty/Creed | **A [Primary]**<br>Equality/Liberation<br>Integration/Wholeness<br>*Life/Self Actualization<br>*Service/Vocation | **B [Primary]**<br>Art/Beauty/As Pure Value<br>*Being Self<br>Construction/New Order<br>Contemplation/ Asceticism<br>*Human Dignity<br>Knowledge/Discovery Insight<br>Presence/Dwelling<br>Ritual/Meaning | **A [Primary]**<br>Harmony/System Personal<br>*Intimacy and solitude as unitive (Union)<br>Truth/Wisdom/Intuitive Insight | **B [Primary]**<br>*Ecority/Beauty Aesthetics<br>*Transcendence/ Global Congruence<br>Harmony/System |
| **A [Means]**<br>Food/Warmth/Shelter<br>**Safety/Survival | **B [Means]**<br>Affection/Physical<br>Discover/Delight<br>Economics/Profits<br>Property/Control<br>Sensory Pleasure/Sex<br>Wonder/Curiosity | **A [Means]**<br>Being Liked<br>Care/Nurture<br>Competition<br>Control/Order/ Discipline<br>Courtesy/Respect<br>Equilibrium<br>Friendship/Belonging<br>Function<br>**Instrumentality<br>Obedience/Duty<br>Prestige/Image<br>Social Affirmation<br>Support (Peer)<br>Tradition | **B [Means]**<br>Achievement/Success<br>Administration/Control<br>Communications<br>Competition<br>Control/Order/ Discipline<br>Criteria/Rationality<br>Design/Pattern/Order<br>Duty/Obligation<br>Economics/Success<br>*Education (Certification)<br>Efficiency/Planning<br>Hierarchy/Propriety/Order<br>Honor<br>**Instrumentality<br>Law/Rule<br>Loyalty/Respect<br>Management<br>Membership/Institution<br>Objectivity<br>Ownership<br>Patriotism/Esteem<br>Productivity<br>Responsibility<br>Rule/Accountability<br>Workmanship/Craft<br>Unity/Solidarity | **A [Means]**<br>Adaptability/Flexibility<br>(Self) Assertion<br>Congruence<br>Decision/Initiation<br>(Self) Directedness<br>**Empathy<br>Equity/Rights<br>Evaluation/Self System<br>Expressiveness/ Freedom<br>Generosity/Service<br>**Health (Personal)<br>**Independence<br>Law/Guide<br>Limitation/Celebration<br>Obedience/Mutual Accountability<br>Power/Authority/ Honesty<br>Relaxation<br>Search/Meaning<br>Sharing/Listening/ Trust | **B [Means]**<br>**Accountability/Mutual Responsibility<br>Community/Supportive<br>Corporation/Construction/New Order<br>Creativity/Ideation<br>Detachment/Solitude<br>Discernment/Communal<br>Education/Knowledge/ Insight<br>Ethics/Accountability/ Values<br>Growth/Expansion<br>Intimacy<br>Justice<br>Mission/Goals<br>Pioneerism/Innovation/ Progress<br>Pluriformity<br>Poverty/Simplicity<br>Recreation/Freesence<br>Research/Originality Knowledge<br>Simplicity/Play<br>Cooperation<br>Faith/Risk | **A [Means]**<br>Community/Personalist<br>**Interdependence<br>Synergy<br>Word | **B [Means]**<br>**Convivial tools/ Intermediate Technology<br>Macro Economics |

** Core Values
**Prime Skill Values

# Discernment of the
# Consciousness Track. Instruction 2

1. First it is necessary to decide which value priorities are **act,** which are **choice** and which are **vision.** This is partly arbitrary. First look at the highest **value** cluster and bracket it. This will be **vision.** Next take the lowest stage of cluster and bracket it—this will be **act.** The center cluster will be **choice** and will normally span only two stages.

Example:

| A | I | B | A | II | B | A | III | B | A | IV | B |
|---|---|---|---|---|---|---|---|---|---|---|---|
| | | security | family belonging | | | service/vocation | | | | | |
| | | | | self-competence | | | | | | | |
| | | | courtesy | | administration/ control | empathy | | | accountability | | interdependence |
| | | | | | management | sharing/ listening/ trust | | | | | |
| | | | | | achievement/ success | | | | cooperation | | |

        **Act**        **Choice**        **Vision**

You can see the main cluster is in IIB/IIIa and was central; so this became **choice.**

Take your consciousness track (page 37) and bracket **act, choice** and **vision.**

2. Discuss the results of your chart with your partner—What patterns do you see in each other's chart?

The following questions will help your discussion:

1. **Vision.** Are your vision values ones in which you have the lowest skills?

2. **Act.** Values are the bottom line. When these are not taken care of, you are most likely to be at your poorest performance. Is this accurate in your situation and if so, what might you do to prevent this?

3. **Choice.** What value are you having the most skill problems with? Look at the consciousness track on page 38 and look at the other values in your **choice** cluster area. Are there other values you wish to **add** to your list on page 37?

## Other Questions and Data to Consider

**Information 1.** When your **choice** cluster is more than **one** stage apart from the **choice** cluster of someone you work with, the communication may be hindered as much as 80 percent.

Q. 1. Do you experience such conflicts or problems with other persons whom you know?

**Information 2.** If your main **choice** values are in Phase II, conflict may arise easily with persons who have phase I or III values.

Q. 2. Do you recognize such difficulties occasionally?

**Information 3.** When your choice cluster is between IIb and IIIa as in the example, conflict often occurs between personal creativity and independence and what the system (corporation) requires.

Q. 3. Are you aware of such conflict?

**Information 4.** Persons whose values cluster in phase III or IIIb/IVa may find it difficult to communicate at other levels.

Q. 4. Do you experience such difficulties?

**Information 5.** Persons whose values are IIIb/IVa and who are highly rational may be misreading their value level, especially if their interpersonal skills are low.

Q. 5. Do you know of such instances? Should you recheck your value level?

## Setting Goals and Objectives.
## Instruction 3

1. Take the long-term values, the primary values from the top of your consciousness track, and prioritize them in the order you feel you can and should manage for the next few months. This will constitute your goal statement. Place them in the first column on the chart on page 41.

If you take your lowest **act** value and prioritize it first, you will get an indication of your lowest operating capability. It is worthwhile to reflect on such a ranking and what it would mean, as an exercise in increasing perspective on how your values ought to be prioritized.

2. Now take your **means** values, the ones at the bottom of the chart, and prioritize them separately as a statement of your **objectives.** Place them on the accompanying chart.

# Personal Discernment Analysis

| Goals—Values | Skills | Qualities | Ethical Dimension |
|---|---|---|---|
| 1. | | | |
| 2. | | | |
| 3. | | | |
| 4. | | | |
| 5. | | | |
| 6. | | | |
| 7. | | | |
| 8. | | | |
| 9. | | | |
| 10. | | | |
| **Objectives—Values** | | | |
| 1. | | | |
| 2. | | | |
| 3. | | | |
| 4. | | | |
| 5. | | | |
| 6. | | | |
| 7. | | | |
| 8. | | | |
| 9. | | | |
| 10. | | | |

## The Personal Discernment Chart.
## Instruction 4

1. Turn now to the three charts in the Appendix:
Appendix A—Skill Analysis Track.
Appendix B—Time Analysis Track.
Appendix C—Ethical Development Track.

2. **Appendix A: Skill Analysis.*** This chart categorizes all the values into their four primary skill areas: **instrumental** or professional and cognitive skills, designated "$I_2$"; **interpersonal** skills or human relations skills, designated "IP"; **imaginal** skills or the ability to create new initiatives and synthesize data into new forms, designated "IM"; and finally **system** skills, or the ability to manage the parts as they relate to the whole, designated "IS."

Simply look up each value on your goals and objective chart, p. 41, and using Appendix A, Skill Analysis Track, see what skill area they fall into and put the designation in the skill column. Example: Empathy—IP; Work/Labor—$I_2$.

3. **Appendix B. Time Analysis.**\* This chart categorizes the values into components of work **W,** work maintenance **WM,** play **P,** play maintenance **PM,** and play freesense **PF.** Again read the values from the previous page on the chart and write the designation under **qualities** in your **personal discernment grid.** Example: Contemplation—PF.

4. **Appendix C.**† **Ethical Development Analysis.**\* As before, read the values and place one of the four ethical designations—**institution**/communal; **ideological; service;** or **dialogical**/legal—in the last column in the **personal discernment analysis.**

You may at this point discuss the chart with your partner to the extent the information is meaningful to you. Consider the following questions:

1. To what extent are the goals and objectives realistic and attainable for you in the immediate future? Do you need to modify them or are you satisfied?

2. In order to live out these goals and objectives, what concrete plan or changes in your use of time and personal relationships are you going to have to make?

3. Does the skill column reflect a need for balance, or do you need to consider developing certain categories of skills?

4. What does the quality column say to you about the work maintenance, play balance in your life?

5. What does the ethical column suggest? Are you happy with what it suggests in your life emphasis?

---

\* See Appendix D to get the information more rapidly.
† The religious version **Values as Discernment** is also available in Appendix C.

## Part 3

# Leadership Analysis, Skill Development and Contract

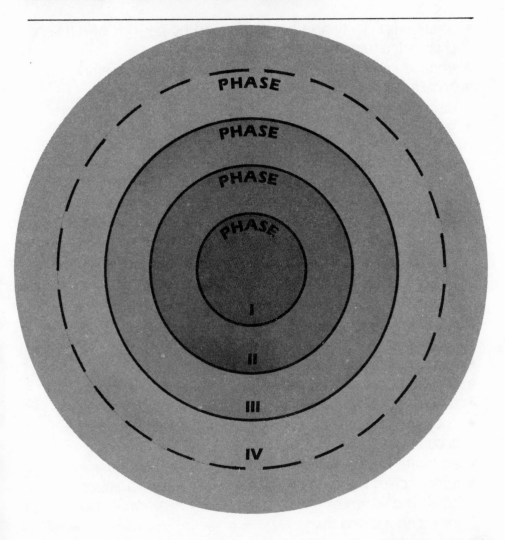

## Skill Inventory

### System Skills

That peculiar blend of imagination, sensitivity and competence which gives rise to the capacity to see all the parts of a system or administration as it is related to the whole. It is the ability to plan and design change in that system (institutions, societies, and bodies of knowledge) so as to maximally enhance the growth of the individual parts. It requires the integration of all the other skills.

Sample Inventory: ability to

- use money as means
- move comfortably with process
- *differentiate in small group setting between interpersonal (person) and the system needs
- clarify group complexity
- *synthesize complex data, statements, and emotional input
- order creatively pressures from internal affairs and societal needs
- speak with clarity and be understood by persons of different phases (cultures and walks of life)
- engage in long term system planning and goal setting
- *make sense of (reflect meaningfully on) apparently disparate data
- set limited design criteria

## Interpersonal Skills

The ability to act with generosity and understanding towards others that flows from a knowledge of oneself. It is the ability to objectify one's own feelings so that cooperation rather than isolation is enhanced.

Sample Inventory: ability to

- show emotion
- identify my feelings accurately
- identify another's feelings accurately
- share emotions
- state anger objectively
- *objectify my and others' feelings and make others accountable
- articulate personal goals
- remain calm in high stress and high anxiety situations
- affirm the worth of others so that they hear what you intend to express
- always complete a communication cycle
- *enable others to see themselves through your 'presence' (empathy)
- *project your imagination into another's world
- be present in death with another
- be creatively aggressive
- cope with conflict
- strategize around polarity

* Key Skills

# Imaginal Skills

That peculiar blend of internal fantasy and feeling (Langer) that enables us to externalize our ideas in an effective and practical manner. It is the ability to see and make sense out of increasing amounts of data. It is the capacity to learn from direct experience, to choose and to act on complex alternatives creatively. As synthesizer, it integrates the other skills.

Sample Inventory: ability to

- *make conscious one's values
- *be able to synthesize new facts
- be able to initiate totally new ideas (association) from seemingly unrelated data
- perceive hidden meaning in standard data
- *be able to dream and imagine new futures—which are possible
- have skills in generating new skills
  —getting group input
  —using consultant help
  —brainstorming
  —"think tank" techniques
- be able to utilize several modes of communication, e.g., verbal/3-D clay/dance


# Instrumental Skills

The peculiar blend of intelligence and manual dexterity that enables one to be professional and competent. It is the ability to manipulate ideas and the immediate external environment. It is the skill of handicrafts, physical dexterity and academic (cognitive) accomplishment.

Sample Inventory: ability to

- read, write and count
- *speak clearly and correctly
- *think logically
- coordinate one's physical self, e.g., drive a car
- master new skills in one's profession, e.g., bookkeeping
- retain primary information processes
- achieve competence in one's labor
- be able to logically integrate and process new technical data
- be able to manage ($XX.00) amount of money per year
- be able to diet, exercise and keep one's body in physical trim

* Key Skills

# Instructions
# Converting Value-Based Goals and
# Objectives Into Personal Skills

## Introduction

1. This is a basic record of the process for converting values into their concomitant skill inventories as it applies to a specific situation.

2. The same process is used for converting goals (primary values) and objectives (means values) into skills, or training programs (educationally grouped skills applied in a teaching environment).

## The Method

1. Take the first long-term goal (primary value) and first objective (means value) for consideration. Given that each value has been defined, make sure that each definition is very specifically related to your institution's purpose, e.g., banking, parish.

2. Using the skill analysis track (Appendix A) see what skill category the first primary value (goal) is in. Employing the instrument, see if any of the other means values are also from this category, and place them on newsprint, as follows:

| Primary Value | Means Values |
|:---:|:---:|
| X | 1. _____ |
| | 2. _____ |
| | 3. _____ |

3. Turn to the Skill Inventory Instrument (page 43) and discuss the skill categories to insure common understanding.

4. Beginning with the first primary and the first means value, brainstorm "activities" you have experienced, especially in reference to your own institution's (company's) needs that are an expression or actualization of the primary and means values you have listed.

Example. Human dignity: Calling together all supervisors for one hour a week to listen to their problems and grievances.

5. List about twenty specific activities. Make sure that each activity could be considered as a specific (occurred in time and place with specific persons) observable performance which is realistic or relevant to your present needs and concerns.

6. Prioritize the activities in terms of those you consider to be the most important during the next planning period. You may wish to group some of the activities together, as being of one common need or experience.

7. Beginning with the first activity and looking at the skill category your values are in, list as many skills as you can that were possibly used in this activity. Begin with the example list and expand to at least fifteen skills.

8. Prioritize the skills, placing the "most needed" skills (not being adequately practiced) at the top of the list, and presently practiced skills at the bottom.

9. Take the first skill and brainstorm, if necessary, on the more specific components of that skill so that the components of the skill are clearly spelled out.

10. Design a specific contract for an individual to develop this skill. The questions raised are:

a. "What behavior would an individual exhibit who has this skill?"

b. "What specific agreement does he have to make with us to see that it is accomplished?"

To design a training program to develop these skills in others, ask:

c. "What training methods shall we employ?"

d. "What external resources do we need, if any?"

11. Having completed the first skill inventory of the first value, you now repeat the same exercise using the following key, developing the second skill inventory for this value.

| System | | |
|---|---|---|
| IS | IS | IP |
| **Imaginal** | | |
| IM | IM | $1_2$ |
| **Interpersonal** | | |
| IP | IP | IM |
| **Instrumental** | | |
| $1_2$ | I2 | IM |

If, for example, the first primary value was "human dignity" then you would have discovered from the instrument that it is a system skill—IS in the above key. You would now brainstorm the same way in skills in the second column in the key above—IP or interpersonal skills.

The exception to the rule is when a value appears in two skill categories on the instrument. Example: Pioneerism.

12. To obtain a comprehensive skill inventory, you now move to the other (means) objective values and repeat the exercise, all in relationship to the first long-term goal.

13. Finally, you move to the second long-term goal and repeat the process.

47

## Part IV

# Leadership Analysis, Leadership Style and Final Contract

### Leadership Style Questionnaire.
### Instruction 1

The two stages of value development point to a different style of leadership each of us exhibits. For example, a person with phase two value, stages IIa and IIb will tend to be an organizational person, whereas a person with Ib and IIa value is going to be more benevolent.

It is our experience that each **level** of leadership raises different questions for the leader manager to ask him or herself. This becomes particularly critical at the middle range of leadership. These questions are particularly helpful in giving general counsel to personnel in hiring or promotional practices. In preparation for the questions:

1. Look at the diagram "The Seven Levels of Leadership Development" (p. 49). Look now at your "Consciousness Track" (p. 37) and identify the **choice area**—in order to

identify your **leader level.** Example: If your choice values were in stages IIb/IIIa you would be designated **leader 4.**

2. Turn now with your partner to the questionnaire for each level and discuss for forty-five minutes. What implications has this for your decision-making and training to be a better leader manager? Remember that a leader is one who influences others. This might mean parent, priest, or salesman.

## The Seven Levels of Leadership Development

| LEADER STAGE | SKILL AND PHASE RANGE LEVEL | WORLD VIEW | LEADER STYLE | FOLLOWER STYLE |
|---|---|---|---|---|
| 1 | I | World as Alien "Alienated Man" | Autocrat Tyrant Dictator | Oppressed Total Dependence |
| 2 | Ib IIa | World as Survival Problem "Preservative Man" | Godfather Benevolent Dictator | Blind Obedient Servant (Means But No End) |
| 3 | II | World as Problem "Organization Man" | Organization Man (Executive) Benevolent Paternalist | Dedicated Servant Organization Loyalist |
| 4 | IIb IIIa | World as Meaning Maker "Communal Man" | Laissez-faire Clarifier Supporter | Leader-Follower Are Confused (Identity Seeker) |
| 5 | III | World as Invention "Independent Man" | Charismatic (Weber) Facilitative Democrat Carpetbagger | Intermediate Peer Participation |
| 6 | IIIb IVa | World as Cooperative Venture "Creator Man" | Leader as Servant Collegial leadership Interdependent Administration | Collegial Participation |
| 7 | IV | World as Mystery Cared For "Man as Prophet" | Leadership Vision | |

MY CHOICE VALUES ARE: _____ STAGES _____

MY LEADER LEVEL IS: _____

## Consciousness Track Analysis: Leadership Style

### Questions By Leadership Level
#### LEVEL I:

1. Are you experiencing a crisis of trust in others? What skills do you need to grow?
2. What educational events are you engaged in?

3. Do you tend to manipulate others? Can you risk trusting others?

4. What are your personal needs, and what can you do to begin to fulfill them?

Note: These questions should be asked of anyone who has any values in phase I.

## LEVEL 2:

1. Do you practice active listening with your workers? What values do they have?

2. Do you take seriously what they tell you?

3. How can you delegate authority more easily?

4. What practical skills do you need to learn? Do you have sufficient administrative skills?

5. Do you spend enough time at home?

6. What are your assumptions about management?

7. How do you get on with people? What could be improved?

## LEVEL 3:

1. What is your work team like?—Or do you have one?

2. What are your main difficulties?

3. What interpersonal skills and accomplishments do you have? What do you need?

4. What is your health like?

5. Do you spend any time in play with your family?

6. What are your personal goals?

7. How much do you share with others?

8. What plans to you have to gain more education?

9. What skills in business administration do you need?

10. What professional skills do you need?

11. Do you know how to plan goals and objectives of a small group—or do you tell them how it is?

12. What are your assumptions about leading?

13. Do you know about human relations development, and what it does do for an organization?

## LEVEL 4: Question of Integration

1. Knowledge Integration.

Do you have good survival skills?

Do you consider it embarrassing to ask others to help you?

Do you need to learn some things?

Do you have sufficient administrative skills?

What are your interpersonal skills like:

50

- Ability to use aggression creatively.
- Ability to empathize.
- Ability to trust, share, and listen.
- Ability to run a small group and clarify feelings as well as cognitive data.

2. Intimacy Integration.

Do you have someone you can share intimately with as a **peer** outside your work? Does your marriage or community need maintenance?

3. Work Integration.

Do you have a work team? Are you building one that meets at least once per week?

4. Peer Integration.

Do you have a professional peer or peers whom you meet regularly with, who are not members of the previous groupings?

**Also** ask some level 5 questions.

**LEVEL 5:**

Add these questions to the level 4 questions.

1. What is your management of time like? Are you at home enough? Do you balance **work** with **play?**

2. What do you do in the way of physical health? And diet? Sports?

3. Are you aware of relaxation, nonattachment and meditation methods? How much time do you spend in these exercises?

4. Are you making an effort to build peer-team consultations and relationships? Is your organization helping you?

5. Do you have sufficient skills with aggression and accountability? Do you have skills in goal-setting, diagnosis and role determination?

Consider some level 6 questions.

**LEVEL 6:** Consider questions at level 4 and 5 and add these.

1. What do I consider servant leadership to be?

2. Am I conscious of my values, the values of my family and peer groups, and do these same values really guide my and our action?

3. Am I living my values? Do I reevaluate myself annually?

4. Do I act congruently in my professional life with my value assumptions?

5. Do I have the correct rhythm in solitude and intimacy?

6. Have I prepared well for retirement and aging? What do I wish to do?

7. Am I current in professional and world affairs?

8. Are my peer groups intact?

9. Do I pay sufficient attention to stages of consciousness in my communications?

10. Am I afraid to risk? What ethical problems do I need to address?

11. Do I continually renegotiate vision?

Having discussed your questions thoroughly with your partner, begin to formulate some questions about your future development.

- What is my health like?
- What are my educational needs?
- Do I play enough?
- Is my family getting sufficient attention from me?

## Writing a Contract.
## Instruction 2

This is a contract that you should do once a year and review every six months to see how you are doing. It summarizes all the elements from all four parts of the **Personal Discernment Analysis.** Be sure each plan is specific, that it is an **observable performance** in time and place, and that it is **realistic** and demands your evaluated initiative.

| Contract Area | Intended Action Plan. Time. Place. Person. |
|---|---|
| Goals<br><br>1. _____<br><br>2. _____<br><br>3. _____<br><br>4. _____<br><br>5. _____ | What I need to do to accomplish my goals:<br><br>_____<br><br>_____<br><br>_____<br><br>_____<br><br>_____ |
| Objectives<br><br>1. _____<br><br>2. _____<br><br>3. _____<br><br>4. _____<br><br>5. _____ | What I need to begin with right away:<br><br>_____<br><br>_____<br><br>_____<br><br>_____<br><br>_____ |

## Contract Area

| Skills | |
|---|---|
| Basic Education<br><br>Administration<br><br>Interpersonal—Listening<br><br>Small Group<br><br>Accountability | The general area I need work in:<br><br><br>What I am prepared to start with: |
| Intimacy/Family | What I need to do outside work:<br><br>Family/Friends, Community and Play: |
| Contract Plan | Intended Action Plan. Time. Place, Person. |
| Work Team and Delegation | What I need in this area: |
| Peer Integration | What professionals outside of work can I meet regularly with? What am I doing or intend to do: |

| Intended Action Plan | |
|---|---|
| Evaluation:<br><br>    Regularity<br><br>    Time/Place | |
| **Additional Contract When Applicable:** | |
| 1. Diet and Physical Exercise | My last physical was:<br><br>My program is: |
| 2. Play and Play/Freesence Activity | |
| 3. Relaxation and Detachment Exercise | |
| 4. Meditation Methods | |
| 5. Reading and Special Studies | |

# Appendix A  Skill Analysis

| | PHASE I — A (Primary/Means) | PHASE I — B (Primary/Means) | PHASE II — A (Primary/Means) | PHASE II — B (Primary/Means) | PHASE III — A (Primary/Means) | PHASE III — B (Primary/Means) | PHASE IV — A (Primary/Means) | PHASE IV — B (Primary/Means) |
|---|---|---|---|---|---|---|---|---|
| **IM** — IMAGINAL (Primary) | Wonder/Awe/Fate | (Self) Delight | Play/Fantasy | | | Art/Beauty/<br>As Pure Value<br>Knowledge/Discovery/<br>Insight | Truth/Wisdom<br>Intuitive Insight | Econty/Beauty/<br>Aesthetics |
| **IM** — IMAGINAL (Means) | | Discovery/Delight<br>Wonder/Curiosity | | Design/Pattern/<br>Order<br>Play/Leisure | Expressiveness/<br>Freedom<br>Search/Meaning | Creativity/Ideation<br>Recreation/Freesence<br>Research/Knowledge<br>Simplicity/Play/<br>Originality | | |
| **IS** — SYSTEMS (Primary) | | | | | **Health (Personal)<br>*Service/Vocation | Being Self<br>Contemplation/<br>Asceticism<br>**Human Dignity<br>Ritual Meaning | Harmony/Personal<br>System | Harmony/<br>Systems<br>Transcendence/<br>Global/<br>Congruence |
| **IS** — SYSTEMS (Means) | | | Equilibrium<br>Social Affirmation<br>Tradition | Hierarchy/Propriety/<br>Order<br>Honor<br>Membership | Expressiveness/<br>Freedom<br>**Independence<br>Law/Guide<br>Obedience/Mutual<br>Accountability<br>Relaxation | Accountability/Mutual<br>Responsibility<br>Community/Supportive<br>Construction/<br>New Order<br>Cooperation<br>Corporation/Construc-<br>tion/New Order<br>Detachment/Solitude<br>Discernment/<br>Communal<br>Ethics/Accountability<br>Values | Community/Person-<br>alist<br>Synergy<br>Interdependence<br>Word | Convivial Tools/<br>Intermediate<br>Technology<br>Macro<br>Economics |

54

I₂

IP

**INSTRUMENTAL:**
A (Primary)
Food/Warmth/Shelter
**Safety/Survival

B (Primary)

B (Means)
Economics/Profits
Property/Control

**INSTRUMENTAL:**
A (Primary)

A (Means)
Function

B (Primary)
*Self Competence/
Confidence
Work/Labor
Worship/Duty/Creed

B (Means)
Achievement/Success
Administration/Control
Communications
Competition
Control/Order
Discipline
Criteria/Rationality
Economics/Success
**Education/
Certification
Efficiency/Planning
Institution/
Management
**Instrumentality
Law/Rule
Membership
Objectivity
Productivity
Rule/Accountability
Workmanship/Craft

**INSTRUMENTAL:**
A (Primary)

A (Means)

B (Primary)
Growth/Expansion
Justice
Mission/Goals
Poverty/Simplicity
Pluriformity
Pioneerism/
Innovation/
Progress

B (Primary)
Contemplation/
Asceticism

B (Means)
Education/Knowledge/
Insight
Ethics/ Accountability/
Values
Simplicity/Play

**INSTRUMENTAL:**
A (Primary)

A (Means)

B (Primary)
Ecority/Beauty/
Aesthetics

B (Means)

**INTERPERSONAL**
A (Primary)
Self Centeredness
Self Preservation

A (Means)

B (Primary)
*Security

B (Means)
Affection/Physical
Sensory Pleasure/Sex

**INTERPERSONAL**
A (Primary)
Self Control
**Family Belonging
*Self Worth

A (Means)
Being Liked/
Appreciated
Care/Nurture
Courtesy/Respect
Friendship/Belonging
Obedience Duty
Prestige/Image
Support/Peer

B (Primary)
Play/Leisure
Unity/Solidarity

B (Means)
Duty/Obligation
Law/Rule
Loyalty/Respect
Management
Ownership
Patriotism/Esteem
Responsibility

**INTERPERSONAL:**
A (Primary)
Equality/Liberation
Integration/Wholeness
*Life/Self
Actualization

A (Means)
Adaptability/Flexibility
(Self) Assertion
Congruence
(Self) Directed/Action
Decision/Initiation
Equity/Rights
Evaluation/Self System
Generosity/Service
Limitation/Celebration
Power/Authority
Honesty
Search/Meaning
Sharing/Listening/Trust

B (Primary)
Presence/Dwelling

B (Means)
Faith/Risk
Intimacy
Responsibility

**INTERPERSONAL:**
A (Primary)
Intimacy and solitude
as unitive (Union)

A (Means)

B (Primary)

B (Means)

# Skills Analysis

IM  Art/Beauty/As Pure Value
Creativity/Ideation
Self/Delight
Discovery/Delight
Ecority/Beauty/Aesthetics
Expressiveness/Freedom
Fantasy/Play
Knowledge/Discovery/Insight
Play/Leisure
Recreation/Freesence
Research/Originality/Knowledge
Search/Meaning
Truth/Wisdom/Intuitive Insight
Wonder/Awe/Fate
Wonder/Curiosity
. . . . . . . . . .
$1_2$ Achievement/Success
Administration/Control
Communications
Competition
(Self) Competence/Confidence
Contemplation/Asceticism
Control/Order/Discipline
Criteria/Rationality
Design/Pattern/Order
Economics/Profits
Economics/Success
Ecority/Beauty/Aesthetics
Education (Certification)
Education/Knowledge/Insight
Efficiency/Planning
Ethics/Accountability/Values
Food/Warmth/Shelter
Function
Instrumentality
Knowledge/Discovery/Insight
Law/Rule
Management
Membership/Institution
Objectivity
Pioneerism/Innovation/Progress
Productivity
Property/Control
Research/Originality/Knowledge

Rule/Accountability
Safety/Survival
Simplicity/Play
Work/Labor
Workmanship/Craft
Worship/Duty/Creed
. . . . . . . . . .
IS  Accountability/Mutual/Responsibility
Being Self
Community/Personalist
Community/Supportive
Construction/New Order
Contemplation/Asceticism
Convivial Tools/Intermediate
    Technology
Cooperation
Corporation/Construction/New Order
Detachment/Solitude
Discernment/Communal
Equilibrium
Ethics/Accountability/Values
Expressiveness/Freedom
Independence
Growth/Expansion
Harmony/Systems
Health (Personal)
Hierarchy/Propriety/Order
Honor
Human Dignity
Interdependence
Justice
Law/Guide
Macro Economics
Mission/Goals
Obedience/Mutual Accountability
Pioneerism/Innovation/Progress
Pluriformity
Poverty/Simplicity
Relaxation
Ritual/Meaning
Service/Vocation
Social Affirmation
Tradition
Synergy

Transcendence/Global/Congruence
Word
. . . . . . . . . .
IP  Adaptability/Flexibility
Affection/Physical
(Self) Assertion
Being Liked
Care/Nurture
(Self) Centeredness
Congruence
(Self) Control
Courtesy/Respect
Decision/Initiation
(Self) Directedness
Duty/Obligation
Empathy
Equality/Liberation
Equity/Rights
Evaluation/Self System
Faith/Risk
Family/Belonging
Generosity/Service
Integration/Wholeness
Intimacy and Solitude as Unitive
Life/Self Actualization
Limitation/Celebration
Loyalty/Respect
Obedience/Duty
Ownership
Patriotism/Esteem
Play/Leisure
Power/Authority/Honesty
Presence/Dwelling
(Self) Preservation
Prestige/Image
Responsibility
Search/Meaning
Security
Sensory Pleasure/Sex
Sharing/Listening/Trust
Support/Peer
Unity/Solidarity
(Self) Worth
. . . . . . . . . .

**KEY:**  IM - Imaginal        $1_2$ - Instrumental
          IS - System        IP - Interpersonal

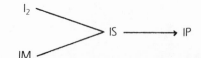

56

## Work
Economics/Profits
Achievement/Success
Criteria/Rationality
Duty/Obligation
Economic/Success
Efficiency/Planning
Function
Instrumentality
Management
Productivity
(Self) Competence/Confidence
Workmanship/Craft
Work/Labor
Accountability/Mutual Responsibility
Corporation/Construction/New Order
Generosity/Service
Growth/Expansion
Human Dignity
Justice
Mission/Goals
Service/Vocation
Convivial Tools/Intermediate Technology
Interdependence
Macro Economics
Instrumentality
Construction/New Order
Worship/Duty/Creed

## Play-Maintenance
Discovery/Delight
Sensory Pleasure/Sex
Wonder/Awe/Fate
Wonder/Curiosity
Family/Belonging
Fantasy/Play
Friendship/Belonging
Ownership
Patriotism/Esteem
Play/Leisure
Prestige/Image
Social Affirmation
Support/Peer
Tradition
Adaptability/Flexibility
(Self) Assertion
Being Self
Empathy
Expressiveness/Freedom
Independence
Life/Self Actualization
Pioneerism/Innovation/Progress
Search/Meaning
Sharing/Listening/Trust
Decision/Initiation
Discernment/Communal

## Maintenance
Affection/Physical
(Self) Centeredness
Self/Delight
Food/Warmth/Shelter
Safety/Survival
Security
Being Liked
(Self) Control
Control/Order/Discipline
Courtesy/Respect
Equilibrium
Unity/Solidarity
(Self) Worth
(Self) Directedness
Equality/Liberation
Equity/Rights
Evaluation/Self System
Health (Personal)
Care/Nurture

## Play
Art/Beauty/As Pure Value
Community/Supportive
Cooperation
Creativity/Ideation
Design/Pattern/Order
Law/Guide
Limitation/Celebration
Presence/Dwelling
Relaxation
Research/Originality/Knowledge
Ritual/Meaning
Simplicity/Play
Ecority/Beauty/Aesthetics
Poverty/Simplicity
Faith/Risk

## Work-Maintenance
| | |
|---|---|
| (Self) Preservation | Obedience/Duty |
| Property/Control | Objectivity |
| Administration/Control | Responsibility |
| Communications | Rule/Accountability |
| Competition | Obedience/Mutual |
| Education (Certification) | Accountability |
| Honor | Pluriformity |
| Law/Rule | Power/Authority/Honesty |
| Loyalty/Respect | Hierarchy/Propriety/Order |
| Membership/Institution | Ethics/Accountability/Values |

## Play-Freesence
Contemplation/Asceticism
Detachment/Solitude
Education/Knowledge/Insight
Recreation/Freesence
Community/Personalist
Harmony/Systems
Intimacy and Solitude as Unitive
Synergy
Transcendence/Global/Confluence
Truth/Wisdom/Intuitive Insight
Word
Congruence

# Time Analysis

| | PHASE I | PHASE II | PHASE III | PHASE IV |
|---|---|---|---|---|
| **WM** | WORK-MAINTENANCE A (Primary) (Self) Preservation — A (Means) — B (Primary) — B (Means) Property/Control | WORK-MAINTENANCE A (Primary) — A (Means) Obedience/Duty — B (Primary) — B (Means) Administration/Control, Communications, Competition, Education (Certification), Honor, Law/Rule, Loyalty/Respect, Membership/Institution, Obedience/Duty, Objectivity, Hierarchy/Propriety/Other, Responsibility, Rule/Accountability | WORK-MAINTENANCE A (Primary) — A (Means) Obedience/Mutual Accountability, Power/Authority/Honesty — B (Means) Pluriformity, Ethics/Accountability/Values | WORK-MAINTENANCE A (Primary) — A (Means) — B (Primary) — B (Means) |
| **M** | MAINTENANCE A (Primary) (Self) Centeredness — A (Means) Food/Warmth/Shelter, Safety/Survival — B (Primary) Self/Delight, Security — B (Means) Affection/Physical | MAINTENANCE A (Primary) (Self) Control, (Self) Worth — A (Means) Being Liked, Courtesy/Respect, Care/Nurture, Equilibrium — B (Primary) Unity/Solidarity — B (Means) Control/Order/Discipline | MAINTENANCE A (Primary) Equality/Liberation, Health (Personal) — A (Means) (Self) Directedness, Equity/Rights, Evaluation/Self System — B (Primary) — B (Means) | MAINTENANCE A (Primary) — A (Means) — B (Primary) — B (Means) |
| **W** | WORK A (Primary) — A (Means) — B (Primary) — B (Means) Economics/Profits | WORK A (Primary) — A (Means) Function — B (Primary) Work/Labor, Worship/Duty/Creed, (Self) Competence/Confidence — B (Means) Achievement/Success, Criteria/Rationality, Duty/Obligation, Economics/Success, Efficiency/Planning, Instrumentality, Management, Productivity, Workmanship/Craft | WORK A (Primary) Service/Vocation — A (Means) Generosity/Service — B (Primary) Human Dignity — B (Means) Accountability/Mutual Responsibility, Construction/New Order, Corporation/Construction/New Order, Growth/Expansion, Justice, Mission/Goals | WORK A (Primary) — A (Means) Interdependence — B (Primary) — B (Means) Convivial Tools/Intermediate Technology, Macro Economics |

58

## Band P

| | |
|---|---|
| PLAY A (Primary) Wonder/Awe/Fate | A (Means) |
| B (Primary) | B (Means) Discovery/Delight Sensory Pleasure/Sex Wonder/Curiosity |
| PLAY A (Primary) | A (Means) |
| B (Primary) | B (Means) Play/Leisure Design/Pattern/Order |
| PLAY A (Primary) | A (Means) Law/Guide Limitation/Celebration Relaxation |
| B (Primary) Art/Beauty/As Pure Value Presence/Dwelling Ritual/Meaning | B (Means) Community/Supportive Cooperation Creativity/Ideation Faith/Risk Poverty/Simplicity Research/Originality/ Knowledge Simplicity/Play |
| PLAY A (Primary) | A (Means) |
| B (Primary) Econy/Beauty/Aesthetics | B (Means) |

## Band PM

| | |
|---|---|
| PLAY-MAINTENANCE A (Primary) | A (Means) |
| B (Primary) | B (Means) |
| PLAY-MAINTENANCE A (Primary) Family/Belonging Fantasy/Play | A (Means) Friendship/Belonging Prestige/Image Social Affirmation Support/Peer Tradition |
| B (Primary) Play/Leisure | B (Means) Ownership Patriotism/Esteem |
| PLAY-MAINTENANCE A (Primary) Life/Self Actualization | A (Means) Adaptability/Flexibility (Self) Assertion Empathy Expressiveness/ Freedom Decision/Initiation Independence Search/Meaning Sharing/Listening/Trust |
| B (Primary) Being Self | B (Means) Discernment/ Communal Pioneerism/ Innovation/ Progress |
| PLAY-MAINTENANCE A (Primary) | A (Means) |
| B (Primary) | B (Means) |

## Band PF

| | |
|---|---|
| PLAY FREESENCE A (Primary) | A (Means) |
| B (Primary) | B (Means) |
| PLAY FREESENCE A (Primary) | A (Means) |
| B (Primary) | B (Means) |
| PLAY FREESENCE A (Primary) Integration/Wholeness | A (Means) |
| B (Primary) Contemplation/ Asceticism Knowledge/Discovery/ Insight | B (Means) Detachment/Solitude Education/Knowledge/ Insight Intimacy Recreation/Freesence |
| PLAY FREESENCE A (Primary) Intimacy and Solitude as Unitive Truth/Wisdom/ Intuitive Insight Word | A (Means) Community/Personalist Congruence Synergy |
| B (Primary) Presence/Other Incarnation Harmony/ Systems | B (Means) Transcendence/Global Confluence |

# Appendix C  Values as Discernment

| | PHASE I | PHASE II | PHASE III | PHASE IV |
|---|---|---|---|---|
| **World view:** | SALVATION from Hell | KINGDOM | RELATIONSHIP | IMMERSION |
| **SELF criteria:** | JUSTIFICATION | CHURCH membership | IMITATION | IDENTIFICATION |
| **CHRIST seen as:** | HEALER | MASTER | FRIEND | LORD |

## COMMUNAL DIMENSION

| Phase | Stage | Values |
|---|---|---|
| PHASE I | Food/Warmth/Shelter Safety/Survival | |
| PHASE I | Family/Belonging | Economics/Profit Property/Control; Control/Order/Discipline, Function, Obedience/Duty, Prestige/Image, Worship/Duty/Creed |
| PHASE II | Play/Leisure | Administration/Control, Competition, Duty/Obligation, Education/Certification, Efficiency/Planning, Honor, Institution/Membership, Instrumentality, Law/Rule, Responsibility, Unity/Solidarity |
| PHASE III | Service/Vocation | Equity/Rights, Law/Guide, Obedience/Mutual Accountability, Power/Authority/Honesty, Self Assertion, (Self) Directedness |
| PHASE III | Construction/New Order | Accountability/Mutual Responsibility, Community/Supportive Cooperation, Presence/Dwelling, Intimacy, Responsibility |
| PHASE IV | Intimacy/Solitude as Unitive | Community/Personalist, Interdependence, Synergy |
| PHASE IV | Harmony/Systems | Macro Economics |

## ESCHATOLOGICAL/CONTEMPLATIVE DIMENSION

| Phase | Values |
|---|---|
| PHASE I | Wonder/Awe/Fate; Fantasy/Play |
| PHASE II | Play/Leisure |
| PHASE III | Life/Self Actualization; Art/Beauty/As Pure Value, Creativity/Ideation, Ritual/Meaning |
| PHASE IV | Intimacy/Solitude as Unitive, Truth/Wisdom, Intuitive/Insight; Ecority/Beauty/Aesthetics, Transcendence/Global confluence |

## AGAPTICAL DIMENSION

**Self Centeredness**

| | | | | |
|---|---|---|---|---|
| Discovery/Delight Wonder/Curiosity | Control/Order/ Discipline Tradition | Achievment/Success Criteria/Rationality Design/Pattern/Order Economics/Success | Evaluation/Self System Health/Personal Search/Meaning | Contemplation/ Asceticism Detachment/Solitude Pioneerism/Innovation/ Progress Recreation/Freesence Research/Originality/ Knowledge |
| Sensory Pleasure/Sex Affection/Physical | Being Liked Care/Nurture Friendship/Belonging | Work/Labor | Integration/Wholeness Service/Vocation | Human Dignity |
| | | Management Productivity Workmanship/Craft Communications | Empathy Generosity/Service Limitation/Celebration | Corporation/Construc- tion/New Order Justice Pluriformity Growth/Expansion |
| | | | | Interdependence |
| | | | | Ecority |

## DIAOLOGICAL/COVENANT DIMENSION

**Self Preservation**

| | | | | |
|---|---|---|---|---|
| (Self) Delight Security | Self control Self worth | Self competence/ Confidence Worship/Duty/Creed | Equality/Liberation | Being self Human Dignity Knowledge/Discovery/ Insight |
| | Courtesy/Respect Equilibrium Social Affirmation Support/Peer | Competition Hierarchy/Propriety/ Order Law/Rule Loyalty/Respect Objectivity Ownership Patriotism/Esteem Rule/Accountability | Adaptability/Flexibility Decision/Initiation Expressiveness/Freedom Faith/Risk Independence Law/Guide Relaxation Sharing/Listening/Trust | Discernment/Communal Education/Knowledge/ Insight Ethics/Accountability/ Values Mission/Goals Poverty/Simplicity |
| | | | Word | Convivial Tools/ Intermediate Technology |

# Values as Ethical Development

| | PHASE I | PHASE II | | PHASE III | | PHASE IV | |
|---|---|---|---|---|---|---|---|
| **World view:** | The Right to Live/Survive | Society Provides | | Conscience must Speak | | Civilization to care for | |
| **Self's criteria:** | Physical Satisfaction | Family Belonging | Social Affirmation/Approval/Achievement | Service/Vocation | Construction/New Order | Intimacy/Solitude as Unitive | Selves seek Global Harmony/Interdependent Action |
| | | | | | | | Harmony/Systems |
| **INSTITUTIONAL/ COMMUNAL** | Economics/Profit Property/Control | Control/Order/ Discipline Function Obedience/Duty Prestige/Image Worship/Duty/Creed | Play/Leisure — Administration/Control Competition Duty/Obligation Education/Certification Efficiency/Planning Honor Institution/Membership Instrumentality Law/Rule Responsibility Unity/Solidarity | Equity/Rights Law/Guide Obedience/Mutual Accountability Power/Authority/ Honesty Self Assertion (Self) Directedness | Construction/ New Order — Accountability/Mutual Responsibility Community/Supportive Cooperation Presence/Dwelling Intimacy Responsibility | | Macro Economics |
| | Food/Warmth/Shelter Safety/Survival | | | | | Intimacy/Solitude as Unitive Truth/Wisdom/ Intuitive/Insight | |
| **IDEOLOGICAL/PHILOSOPHICAL** | | Fantasy/Play | Play/Leisure | Life/Self Actualization | Art/Beauty/As pure value Creativity/Ideation Ritual/Meaning | | Econty/Beauty/ Aesthetics Transcendence/Global confluence |
| | Wonder/Awe/Fate | | | | | | |

**SERVICE/LOVE**

Self Centeredness

**DIALOGICAL/LEGAL/COVENANT**

Self Preservation

| | | | | | |
|---|---|---|---|---|---|
| Discovery/Delight Wonder/Curiosity | Control/Order/ Discipline Tradition | Achievement/Success Criteria/Rationality Design/Pattern/Order Economics/Success | Evaluation/Self System Health/Personal Search/Meaning Congruence | Contemplation/ Asceticism Detachment/Solitude Pioneerism/Innovation/ Progress Recreation/Freeesence Faith/Risk Research/Originality/ Knowledge Simplicity/Play | |
| Sensory Pleasure/Sex Affection/Physical | Being Liked Care/Nurture Friendship/Belonging | Work/Labor | Integration/Wholeness Service/Vocation | Human Dignity | Ecority |
| | | Management Productivity Workmanship/Craft Communications | Empathy Generosity/Service Limitation/Celebration | Corporation/Construc- tion/New Order Justice Pluriformity Growth/Expansion | Interdependence / Convivial Tools/ Intermediate Technology |
| [Self] Delight Security | Self Control Self Worth | Self Competence/ Confidence Worship/Duty/Creed | Equality/Liberation | Being Self Human Dignity Knowledge/Discovery/ Insight | |
| | Courtesy/Respect Equilibrium Social Affirmation Support/Peer | Competition Hierarchy/Propriety/ Order Law/Rule Loyalty/Respect Objectivity Ownership Patriotism/Esteem Rule/Accountability | Adaptability/Flexibility Decision/Initiation Expressiveness/Freedom Faith/Risk Independence Law/Guide Relaxation Sharing/Listening/Trust | Discernment/Communal Education/Knowledge/ Insight Ethics/Accountability/ Values Mission/Goals Poverty/Simplicity | Word |

# Appendix D
# Personal Discernment Analysis: Coding System

The following charts are offered as a rapid way of completing the chart on page 41. Each value has been coded for skills, qualities and ethical dimension using the following codes:

On the instruments labeled "Values as Discernment" or "Ethical Development", the codes will be as follows:

**Skills:**

| | |
|---|---|
| Instrumental skills: | $I_2$ |
| Interpersonal skills: | IP |
| Imaginal skills: | IM |
| System skills: | IS |

**Qualities:**

| | |
|---|---|
| Work: | W |
| Maintenance: | M |
| Work-Maintenance: | WM |
| Play Maintenance: | PM |
| Play: | P |
| Play Freesence: | PF |

**Ethical Dimensions:**

Where it reads
Communal Dimension
or, Institutional Communal: CI
Eschatological/Contemplative Dimension
or, Ideological/Philosophical: EI
Agapitical Dimension
or, Service/Love: S
Dialogical/Covenant Division
or, Dialogical/Legal/Covenant: CL

| Values | Skills | Qualities | Ethical Dimension | Values | Skills | Qualities | Ethical Dimension |
|---|---|---|---|---|---|---|---|
| 1. Accountability/Mutual Responsibility | IS | W | CI | 61. Human Dignity | IS | W | S |
| 2. Achievement/Success | $I_2$ | W | EI | 62. Independence | IP | PM | CL |
| 3. Adaptability/Flexibility | IP | PM | CL | 63. Instrumentality | $I_2$ | W | CI |
| 4. Administration/Control | $I_2$ | WM | CI | 64. Integration/Wholeness | IP | PF | S |
| 5. Affection/Physical | IP | M | S | 65. Interdependence | IS | W | S |
| 6. Art/Beauty/As Pure Value | IM | P | EI | 66. Intimacy | IP | PF | CI |
| 7. (Self) Assertion | IP | PM | CI | 67. Intimacy and Solitude as Unitive | IP | PF | EI |
| 8. Being Liked | IP | M | S | 68. Justice | IS | W | S |
| 9. Being Self | IS | PM | CL | 69. Knowledge/Discovery/Insight | $I_2$ | PF | CL |
| 10. Care/Nurture | IP | M | S | 70. Law/Guide | IS | P | CI |
| 11. (Self) Centeredness | IP | M | S | 71. Law/Rule | $I_2$ | WM | CL |
| 12. Communications | $I_2$ | WM | S | 72. Life/Self Actualization | IP | PM | EI |
| 13. Community/Personalist | IS | PF | CI | 73. Limitation/Celebration | IP | P | S |
| 14. Community/Supportive | IS | P | CI | 74. Loyalty/Respect | IP | WM | CL |
| 15. Competition | $I_2$ | WM | CI | 75. Macro Economics | IS | W | CI |
| 16. (Self) Competence/Confidence | $I_2$ | W | CL | 76. Management | $I_2$ | W | S |
| 17. Congruence | IP | PF | EI | 77. Membership/Institution | $I_2$ | WM | CI |
| 18. Construction/New Order | IS | W | S | 78. Mission/Goals | IS | W | CL |
| 19. Contemplation/Asceticism | $I_2$ | PF | EI | 79. Obedience/Duty | IP | WM | CL |
| 20. (Self) Control | IP | M | CL | 80. Obedience/Mutual Accountability | IS | WM | CI |
| 21. Control/Order/Discipline | $I_2$ | M | EI | 81. Objectivity | $I_2$ | WM | CL |
| 22. Convivial Tool/Intermediate Technology | IS | W | S | 82. Ownership | IP | PM | CL |
| 23. Cooperation | IS | P | CI | 83. Patriotism/Esteem | IP | PM | CL |
| 24. Corporation/Construction/New Order | IS | W | S | 84. Pioneerism/Innovation/Progress | IS | PM | EI |
| 25. Courtesy/Respect | IP | M | CL | 85. Play/Leisure | IP | P | CI |
| 26. Creativity/Ideation | IM | P | EI | 86. Poverty/Simplicity | IS | P | CL |
| 27. Criteria/Rationality | $I_2$ | W | EI | 87. Pluriformity | IS | WM | S |
| 28. (Self) Delight | IM | M | CL | 88. Power Authority/Honesty | IP | WM | CI |
| 29. Detachment/Solitude | IS | PF | EI | 89. Presence/Dwelling | IP | P | EI-CI |
| 30. Decision/Initiation | IP | PM | CL | 90. (Self) Preservation | IP | WM | CL |
| 31. Design/Pattern/Order | $I_2$ | P | EI | 91. Prestige/Image | IP | PM | CI |
| 32. (Self) Directedness | IP | M | CI | 92. Productivity | $I_2$ | W | S |
| 33. Discovery/Delight | IM | PM | EI | 93. Property/Control | $I_2$ | WM | CI |
| 34. Discernment/Communal | IS | PM | CL | 94. Recreation/Freesence | IM | PF | EI |
| 35. Duty/Obligation | IP | W | CI | 95. Relaxation | IS | P | CI |
| 36. Economics/Profit | $I_2$ | W | CI | 96. Research/Originality/Knowledge | IM | P | EI |
| 37. Economics/Success | $I_2$ | W | EI | 97. Responsibility | IP | WM | CI |
| 38. Ecority/Beauty/Aesthetics | IM | P | EI-S | 98. Ritual/Meaning | IS | P | EI |
| 39. Education/Certification | $I_2$ | WM | CI | 99. Rule/Accountability | $I_2$ | WM | CL |
| 40. Education/Knowledge/Insight | $I_2$ | PF | CL | 100. Safety/Survival | $I_2$ | M | CI |
| 41. Efficiency/Planning | $I_2$ | W | CI | 101. Search/Meaning | IM | PM | EI |
| 42. Empathy | IP | PM | S | 102. Security | IP | M | CL |
| 43. Equilibrium | IS | M | CL | 103. Sensory Pleasure/Sex | IP | PM | S |
| 44. Equality/Liberation | IP | M | CL | 104. Service/Vocation | IS | W | S |
| 45. Equity/Rights | IP | M | CI | 105. Sharing/Listening/Trust | IP | PM | CL |
| 46. Ethics/Accountability/Values | $I_2$ | WM | CL | 106. Simplicity/Play | $I_2$ | P | EI |
| 47. Evaluation/Self System | IP | M | EI | 107. Social Affirmation | IS | PM | CL |
| 48. Expressiveness/Freedom | IM | PM | CL | 108. Support Peer | IP | PM | CL |
| 49. Faith/Risk | IP | P | CL | 109. Synergy | IS | PF | CI |
| 50. Family/Belonging | IP | PM | CL | 110. Tradition | IS | PM | EI |
| 51. Fantasy/Play | IM | PM | EI | 111. Transcendence/Global Confluence | IS | PF | EI |
| 52. Food/Warmth/Shelter | $I_2$ | M | CI | 112. Truth/Wisdom/Intuitive Insight | IM | PF | EI |
| 53. Friendship/Belonging | IP | PM | S | 113. Unity/Solidarity | IP | M | CI |
| 54. Function | $I_2$ | W | CI | 114. Wonder/Awe/Fate | IM | PM | EI |
| 55. Generosity/Service | IP | W | S | 115. Wonder/Curiosity | IM | PM | EI |
| 56. Growth/Expansion | IS | W | S | 116. Word | IS | PF | CL |
| 57. Harmony/System | IS | PF | CI | 117. Work/Labor | $I_2$ | W | S |
| 58. Health/Personal | IS | M | EI | 118. Workmanship/Craft | $I_2$ | W | S |
| 59. Hierarchy/Propriety/Order | IS | WM | CL | 119. Worship/Duty/Creed | $I_2$ | W | CL |
| 60. Honor | IS | WM | CI | 120. (Self) Worth | IP | M | CL |